ON YOUR OWN

OTHER BOOKS BY THE AUTHOR

The Craft of Corporate Journalism
Fisher Island

ON YOUR OWN

A GUIDE TO WORKING HAPPILY, PRODUCTIVELY & SUCCESSFULLY FROM HOME

Lionel L. Fisher

PRENTICE HALL
Englewood Cliffs, New Jersey 07632

Prentice-Hall International (UK) Limited, *London*
Prentice-Hall of Australia Pty. Limited, *Sydney*
Prentice-Hall Canada, Inc., *Toronto*
Prentice-Hall Hispanoamericana, S.A., *Mexico*
Prentice-Hall of India Private Limited, *New Delhi*
Prentice-Hall of Japan, Inc., *Tokyo*
Simon & Schuster Asia Pte. Ltd., *Singapore*
Editora Prentice-Hall do Brasil, Ltda., *Rio de Janeiro*

©1995 *by*
Lionel L. Fisher

Most of the homeworkers depicted in this book are real.
A few are composite characters.

10 9 8 7 6 5 4 3 2 1

Library of Congress Cataloging-in Publication Data

Fisher, Lionel L.
    On your own: : a guide to working happily, productively &
successfully at home / Lionel L. Fisher.
        p. cm.
    Includes bibliographical references and index.
    ISBN 0-13-031287-8
    1. Home-based businesses. 2. Self-employed. 3. New business
enterprises. 4. Small business. I. Title.
HD2333.F57 1994   94-36443
658'.041—dc20   CIP

ISBN 0-13-031287-8

PRENTICE HALL
Career & Personal Development
A division of Simon & Schuster
Englewood Cliffs, New Jersey 07632

Printed in the United States of America

This book is dedicated to my favorite people: Those who are willing to risk, especially those who have risked and failed, and are willing to risk again. And for Madeline, Mike, Andy, Jane, Nancy, and Lisa.

ACKNOWLEDGMENTS

If only a book was as much fun to write as its acknowledgment page! This is where an author gets to thank the individuals who believed in his book long before it became one. My gratitude, then, to these special people who were indispensible to *On Your Own*:

To Ellen Schneid Coleman, with whom it all started. She saw the book long before it became one. Thank you for your hard work and patience.

To Marsha Weber, whom I expect to be canonized any day now as patron saint of Pacific Northwest wordsmiths. As a free-lance writer, I have long relied on the kindness of librarians. I love them all, but I adore this Nightingale of the downtown Portland book vaults. Not a single time during my endless research forays did she fail to help me, all the while radiating encouragement and unremitting good cheer.

To Sue Hurlbut, whom I initially contacted for a few quotes and wound up going back to again and again because of her boundless enthusiasm for the book and for her variegated contributions to these pages. I have no doubt she is destined to become the Hillary Clinton of professional organizers.

To Patricia Megan Pingree, whom I instantly recognized as a kindred spirit. She has been a kind, willing, tireless source of information and insight, and should be writing books herself.

To Alexandra Kristall, poet and dancer, another kindred spirit whose input and support made this a much better book than it would have been without her avid interest.

To my (not so) old friend Wendy Hughson, who gives an incredible good read.

To Judy Night, my new friend at the beach, whose babysitting of Buddy Holly during a critical time proved invaluable.

To my other new friend, Joleen Colombo, whose contributions in the eleventh hour were magnificent.

To Geoff McGuire, my longtime best friend, creative cohort, and the finest client a freelance writer could wish. His lucrative assignments hauled my financial fat out of the fire more times than I care to remember during the many months of pulling this book together. And I am grateful, as always, to his decidedly better half, Lisa.

Finally, to Jane—ever supportive, indulgent, eager to help, and the best editor I know.

Thank you all.

Lionel L. Fisher

CONTENTS

INTRODUCTION 1

CHAPTER ONE

AT HOME WITH YOUR JOB: MAKING IT WORK FOR YOU 13

What to Expect When You Get Off the Fast Track • Discipline, Determination • Work Defines Us • Acknowledging Ingrained Traits • The Upside and Flipside of Being On Your Own • Balancing Opposing Forces • Is Being On Your Own Right for You? A Self-Assessment Test • Making the Grade • What It Takes to Be On Your Own

CHAPTER TWO

TUNING YOUR PSYCHIC ENGINE: BEING YOUR OWN MECHANIC 25

What Makes You Tick? Exceptions Make the Rule • Pick Your Style • Lift the Hood • Preventive Maintenance • How to Keep

Your Psychic Engine Running Smoothly • What's Important to You: Your Personal Pie Chart

CHAPTER THREE

GETTING A FAST START: OUTRACING MENTAL ROADBLOCKS 33

Jump Right In • Pick Up Where You Left Off: Make the Most of Yesterday's Energy • How to Outfox Your Inertia • Reward Yourself: Dangle a Carrot • Program Your Starts: Pavlovian Responses to Start Your Day • Eight Ways to Get Under Way Quickly

CHAPTER FOUR

BUILDING SELF-DISCIPLINE, MOTIVATION EMOTIONAL TENACITY 41

Self-Discipline: Vital As Air When You're On Your Own • Know Yourself: How Much Self-Motivation Do You Require? • Ex-marine Tells How • Learn to Say No • Beware Desire to Belong • Five Ways to Graciously, but Effectively, Say "No!" to Others • Overcoming Self-Doubt • How to Create Belief in Yourself • How to Say "Yes!" to Yourself

CHAPTER FIVE

DEVELOPING ORGANIZATIONAL SKILLS: MAXIMIZING PRODUCTIVITY 53

Small Steps That Lead to Big Organization • Organization Is Your Rudder • Organization: Your Passport to Time Management • Seven Ways to Keep Organized • How to Do More with Less Effort

• Handy Is Dandy • Make Molehills out of Mountains • Create Checklists • Keep Things Simple • Housebreaking the Paper Lion

CHAPTER SIX

AN OFFICE IS NOT A HOME: NECESSARY BOUNDARIES 65

Home and Office: How *Not* to Blur the Boundaries • Your Place of Business: Make It Professional • Mental Commuting • Creating a Workplace That Suits Your Needs • Creating Mental Boundaries • Creating Physical Boundaries • On Your Own: Away from Home • The Benefits of Working Away from Home • Too Close to Comfort • Some Must Modify the Dream • For Some Work Ethics, Spartan Is Better than Luxurious • The Four Walls of Your Mind • Structuring a Work Zone • Dress for Success • Maintain Regular Hours • Stay Flexible • Don't Mix Work and Leisure • Strategic Withdrawals • Knowing When to Quit • Leave Promptly

CHAPTER SEVEN

EXTINGUISHING PROCRASTINATION: LIGHTING A FIRE UNDER YOURSELF 81

Snap the Elastic Deadline • Don't Live for Tomorrow • Sometimes It's Smart to Procrastinate—What to Do When It's Not • Handle the Problem! • Reward Yourself for a Job Well Done • Don't Accept Substitutes • Shun Creative Malingering • What to Do When Cures Become Problems • What Type of Procrastinator Are You? • Procrastination's Tell-Tale Tip-Offs • How to Combat Procrastination • Respect Your Work Ethic • Fight Your Own Battle • Ten Ways to Kick Procrastination • Turning CAN'Ts into CANs • Clear the Way for Action • Assign Each Task a Deadline • Make a Daily To-Do List • Jump-Start the Day • Gearing for Battle • Preparation Is Everything • What to Do When You Can't Get Going • Never Surrender • Lose a Battle, Win the War • Dissolving Writer's Block

CHAPTER   EIGHT

BEFRIENDING SOLITUDE: HOW TO BE ALONE, NOT LONELY 103

Can You Handle Solitude? • The Emotional Cost of Freedom • Making Your Own World • What to Do When There's No One But You • How to Nurture Yourself • Tempering Solitude • Creative Solutions: Alone in the Company of Others • Enter the Portable Office • Nomadic Workers • Facing Your Loneliness • Recognizing the Triggers of Loneliness and the Benefits of Being On Your Own • How to Handle the Transition to Working Alone • Sharing the Bad Stuff • Necessary Growth • Using Solitude Well • How to Be Alone, Not Lonely • Talk Out Loud If It Helps • Engage in Active Solitude • Hold Your Ground

CHAPTER   NINE

THE IDEAL HOME OFFICE: PERSONAL FIT IS EVERYTHING 123

Creating the Ideal Home Office • Questions to Ask Yourself • Are Right-Brain/Left-Brain Considerations Important in Selecting Office Furniture? • Quick Tips for Designing a Home Office on a Limited Budget • Before You Buy Checklist • How to Organize Your Professional Home Office

CHAPTER   TEN

ALL IN THE FAMILY: WORKING ALONE TOGETHER 135

Handling Home/Office Career/Family Conflict • What to Do When the Kids Are at Home • How to Alternate Responsibilities • Don't Become Your Own Worst Enemy • What to Do When You

Both Work at Home • Accommodating Different Work Styles • Respect and Communication: Two Keys to Success • Family Time/Work Time: Separate Is Essential • Recognize Potential Conflicts Before They Occur • How to Handle Conflict When It Does Occur • Five Essentials When You Work Alone Together

C H A P T E R   E L E V E N

TALKING YOURSELF INTO SUCCESS: SELF-ACTUALIZATION TECHNIQUES 153

Make It Happen: Rehearse Your Success • How to Create a Mood for Success • Mental Drills Plus Practice Equal Success • How to Talk Yourself into Success • Consult Your Inner Self • Relax Your Way to Success • On Your Own with Guided Imagery • Learning to Relax • Painting the Pictures • Consulting Your Advisor • Encountering Emotion • Using Imagery to Achieve Peak Performance • Firewalking on Cool Thoughts • Scripting Your Success • Script #1: Visualizing Your Success • Script #2: Defeating Procrastination • Script #3: Befriending Solitude • Script #4: Building Self-Confidence • Script #5: Tapping Your Wellspring • Pick Up This Marvelous Tool and Use It

C H A P T E R   T W E L V E

DEVELOPING SURVIVAL SKILLS: WHAT IT TAKES TO BE "ON YOUR OWN" 181

The Most Important Trait Home Aloner's Possess • The Difference Is Mental • A Passion for Life • On Your Own, But Not Alone • Nine Essential Strengths • Taking Pride in Succeeding On Your Own • Celebrate Yourself

BIBLIOGRAPHY 193

INDEX 203

INTRODUCTION

The inspiration, when it finally came, found me in my favorite position: Flat on my back, in the middle of my second nap of the day.

"Get up," said the tiny voice in my head as a light bulb switched on. "You have a book to write."

I rolled over. I didn't need anything else to procrastinate about. I already had plenty of work I was ignoring.

The voice followed me into the kitchen. "You have a *book*," it said, making me feel like Ray Kinsella in his Iowa cornfield.

I usually get hungry when I'm feeling guilty, so I made lunch. When I'd finished eating, the voice still hadn't gone away.

"Do a book on what it's like, what it's *really* like, to work alone," the voice persisted.

"Tell people how to stay focused, motivated, organized, purposeful, productive, and happy on their own.

"Tell them how to keep psychologically centered and emotionally afloat when there's no one to hold you up but *you*.

"What it takes to hang in there all by yourself, day after solitary day, without the company, direction, camaraderie, and support of co-workers and supervisors.

"Tell them about the best and toughest job in the world: Being your own boss.

"You ought to know," the voice took a cheap shot. "You've worked alone most of your life and you're still struggling."

"So what?" I countered brilliantly. "I wouldn't trade it for the world."

Nearly 40 Million On Their Own

I wouldn't trade it, and neither would at least 39 million others. That's the number of Americans LINK Resources Corporation estimated last year, who work full-time or part-time from home. They represent a 9.4 percent increase over 1991. And their ranks will continue to grow: According to BIS Strategic Decisions, a Massachusetts market research/consulting firm, American home-workers will total nearly 43 million by 1995.

Alvin Toffler goes even further. In his book, *The Third Wave*, in which he coins the phrase "electronic cottage," Toffler predicts that one day up to half the people in the country will spend all or part of their working lives at home.

Wives do it, husbands do it, most of them apart, some side by side. They do it in living rooms, bedrooms, kitchens, basements, alcoves, attics, garages, walk-in closets, nooks, and crannies of houses and apartments. They do it out of car trunks, in hideaway offices, sailboats, trailers, studios, bungalows, ski chalets, RVs, you name it. Wherever a desk, worktable, drafting board, easel, computer, copier, fax, modem, or telephone will fit.

The 21st Century Office

The "virtual" office has burst onto the scene. It's not really a place, notes Phil Patton of *The New York Times*, but a "nonplace." More of an idea, actually a work style whose time has come. It is the 21st century office, with no particular address, not even parameters.

"For years now, office workers have been begging for flexible time and the right to work at home," writes Patton. "Now, more and more employers are saying yes. Companies committing themselves to the virtual office are practically pushing their employees out the door and into cars and spaces designed, like hotels, for drop-in work."

To trim costs and promote productivity, a growing number of companies are cutting their sales staff's office space, confirms *Sales & Marketing Management* magazine, equipping them with laptop computers, cellular phones, and portable printers, then sending them on the road to create their own makeshift offices.

Reports Patton: "The virtual office or "V.O." as its proponents call it, comes with sometimes jolting side effects, like answered prayers, and workers are learning to adapt with a mixture of enthusiasm and bafflement."

Advertising account executive Peggy Roswell likens it to "going from high school to college, where no one is around to make sure you go to class."

Roswell now feels, "It's no longer my life fitting into my work, but my work fitting into my life."

Who Works Alone?

Says LINK, a New York-based International Data Group company, the estimated 39 million Americans who currently work alone include:

12.1 MILLION FULL-TIME SELF-EMPLOYED HOMEWORKERS. Comprising almost a third of the total work-at-home population, these individuals typically operate one-person businesses, or they freelance as consultants and contract workers. Most of them are professionals and entrepreneurs.

11.7 MILLION PART-TIME SELF-EMPLOYED HOMEWORKERS. These people hold multiple jobs and work from their homes part of the time. This segment registered an 11 percent increase over 1991, reflecting the economic recession's impact on the sizable number of Americans seeking to supplement their regular incomes.

6.6 MILLION TELECOMMUTERS. These are company employees who work in their homes either part-time or full-time during normal business hours. For the second straight year, says LINK, this group expanded more than all other work-at-home segments, underscoring the growing need for flexibility in the workplace.

Telecommuting is an effective way to maintain job productivity while addressing employees' quality-of-life concerns as well as the nation's mounting traffic congestion and air pollution problems.

8.6 MILLION CORPORATE AFTER-HOURS HOMEWORKERS. These are company employees who use personal computers, modems, fax machines, and extra phone lines to do company work at home after normal business hours. This segment decreased by 2 million in 1992 as employees, facing salary cuts and layoffs, simply cut back the extra hours they were willing to give their employers. Also, some of the previous year's after-hours homeworkers became telecommuters or began moonlighting to earn extra income.

Why They Work Alone

Their numbers are large and proliferating, but why? Respondents of *Home Office Computing*'s annual reader poll gave these reasons:

1. I wanted to be my own boss. (72%)
2. I wanted less routine in my life. (56%)
3. I wanted to change my life. (43%)
4. I wanted to do more interesting work. (41%)
5. I disliked the corporate world. (35%)
6. I wanted to spend more time with my family. (33%)
7. I wanted to make more money. (29%)
8. I had a great idea for a business. (25%)
9. I'd gone as far as I could at the company I worked for. (23%)

Sound familiar?

They do to Duke Castle. The first six are all part of why he left a successful high-tech company to head his own business planning firm. "I wanted to find something more meaningful in life," sums up the Stanford MBA.

There's another word for what Castle did, coined by Amy Saltzman, a *U.S. News & World Report* editor and author of a 1992 book on a phenomenon sociologists are heralding as a hot new trend. "Downshifting," Saltzman calls it: The deliberate pursuit of greater personal fulfillment on a slower, more private professional track.

Then there are the 10 million business managers and professionals between the ages of 35 and 45 who are entering two of life's passages at once—middle age and parenthood. It's happening for the first time in American history. Not until the mid-1980s did the percentage of parents among baby boomers crest at 50 percent. Sixty percent of them now have children.

For these middle-aged boomers, confronted with their vulnerability and the desire to pass along the right values to their children, quality-of-life choices have become paramount considerations.

As a result, many boomers are exiting the corporate fast lanes, inventing new ways to live and work. And attempting to do it at home with their families.

"A path with heart," as Carlos Castaneda puts it.

Working Alone: The Wave of the Future

Other statistics offer evidence that the countercultural migration isn't just this year's fad. According to a recent Gallup poll, most baby boomers claim they won't increase the time they spend at work in the next five years. Fifty percent of boomer women and 37 percent of the men expect to cut back on their work hours.

At the same time, a Yankelovich Monitor survey of consumer behavior discloses that Americans are more willing than ever to make job changes and to take pay cuts in exchange for more leisure time or self-satisfying work.

"Whether by choice or misfortune," observes *Adweek's* Sarah Mahoney, "the 35-to-54 demographic is undergoing a major upheaval. Men are looking at everything, from their careers to their family, in a new light."

Nor is the emerging generation exempt. "Perhaps in response to the glitz and glitter of the 1980s," Jann S. Wenner, editor and publisher of *Rolling Stone*, commented in *Advertising Age* magazine, "twentysomethings in 1993 are looking beyond the figures on their pay stubs when measuring personal success.

"They want work that makes them feel that they are accomplishing something meaningful. They want a lifestyle that affords plenty of free time to spend with family and friends. They want to live in communities where people know and support one another. They want the security of family and strong relationships, the security of community, and the security of knowing that they are making a positive contribution to society."

And many of them are seeking it on their own.

Balancing Profit and Lifestyle

Business and industry, therefore, can expect executives and workers alike to pressure their employers for more flexible hours, shorter workdays and workweeks, job sharing, flex-time and telecommuting, along with the elimination of overtime and the establishment of child-care centers, elderly care assistance, extended family leaves, periodical sabbaticals, and simply more time off. For decades now, Americans have envied the generous vacation time negotiated by employees in many European countries.

As a matter of fact, the trend toward telecommuting, claims John Niles, who coined the word in 1973, is not only nationwide, it's worldwide. "Strangely, the United States is lagging," says Niles, a Southern California management consultant and national expert on the subject. "Telecommuting is more available in Europe and Australia." The number of telecommuters in the country is growing at about 20 percent a year, he claims.

"The forward-thinking American companies," predicts business consultant Castle, "will find ways to balance profits with stronger, deeper commitments to their employees' lifestyles and communities. The challenge is reconciling these values with the need to make a profit, especially in economic hard times."

As the pendulum of social change swings from the "Gimme, gimme!" greed of the 1980s to the decade of the family the 1990s has become, there will be winners and losers. But this change, like all change, is inevitable.

And nowhere is it more evident than in the swelling ranks of Americans riding Toffler's Third Wave into their electronic cottages.

What They Do Now

For what kind of work are these men and women trading today's crowded corporate tracks and gridlocked commuter lanes? These are the *top 10 home-based occupations of the 1990s,* according to *Home Office Computing*:

1. Consulting
2. Computer Services/Programming
3. Business Support/Services
4. Financial Support/Services
5. Independent Sales
6. Graphic, Visual, and Fine Arts
7. Writing
8. Marketing/Advertising
9. Construction/Repair
10. Real Estate

BIS Strategic Decisions further defines the various types of homeworkers as:

New Entrepreneurs: Sole proprietors of a business, who account for all or most of their household's income.

Contributors: Who run a business from home but have other sources of income as well.

Dilettantes: Who contribute less than 25 percent of their household's total income and typically are less interested in financial rewards than in artistic or creative fulfillment.

Corporate Beavers: Employed by a regular place of business but who bring work home to do after hours and on weekends.

Telecommuters: Traditional employees, some of whom work exclusively from home; most of this group, however, spend more time in their corporate offices than at home.

Chairpersons: Principals or senior executives of their firms, who have the luxury of choosing to stay home and work occasionally rather than go to the office.

New Directions in Home Work

However defined, more and more Americans are choosing to work for themselves and by themselves. In growing numbers they are trading security, conventional success, and a lavish standard of living for personal fulfillment and what they perceive to be a better quality of life.

In 1986, according to the latest Bureau of Labor Statistics figures, roughly 10 million workers, including some 4.6 million women, swapped old occupations for new.

A Yankelovich Monitor survey reveals that the share of women who feel having "enough money" would get them to quit work permanently was 35 percent in 1987. That figure dipped to 33 percent in 1988, rose to 38 percent in 1989 and soared to 56 percent in 1990.

The share of men who described their job as a "career" slipped from 50 percent in 1989 to 48 percent in 1990.

Early retirement is becoming the rule rather than the exception.

Demographic studies strongly favor the work-at-home trend. The overwhelming indication is that baby boomers and younger adults are far less enthusiastic about conventional work than the generations before them. What's more, boomers are at the age when they are most likely to work at home. In 1994, the median age of homeworkers was 38—also the median age of baby boomers.

Joseph Plummer, managing director of Paine Webber/Young & Rubicam Ventures in New York, provides a few more interesting statistics. Among Harvard MBAs graduating between 1942 and 1978, 30 percent are now self-employed. In contrast, 87 percent of the class of 1984 said they planned to start or run their own companies.

"Even if as many as half of them never do so," notes Plummer, "this class represents a 50 percent increase in entrepreneurship over the past 40 years."

Getting a Life

The once-slim ranks of artists and writers are awash in a flood of "homepreneurs," "homesteaders," and "flexworkers." They are the men and women in today's electronic cottages, using new technology to pursue lucrative, fulfilling careers: Americans who choose to work "differently," who have opted to "get a life" instead of just another job, who have traded subways, buses, and freeways for a downstairs commute.

In a communiqué to the American people during his last year in office, George Bush commended these men and women: "If even a small segment of our work force spent one or two days a week working from home or from a satellite work center, we would not only save immense amounts of time and gasoline but also enjoy a significant reduction in traffic congestion and in air pollution.

"As American commerce moves into the future, we should remember that sometimes the best policy is not moving people, but moving their work."

"A number of forces are converging to cause a 'workquake' in our society," says John Knowlton, publisher/editor of *Home-Based Business News*, a Portland, Oregon-based publication that covers the nation's growing home-business community. "These forces will forever change the way we conduct our business lives."

Undeniably, the low cost of computers and other new technology has made it infinitely easier to set up a home office and to telecommute to work.

Also, "downsizing" and "decruiting" have become the corporate watchwords of the 1990s, says Knowlton, who observed the developing homeoffice trend for 20 years as a newspaper editor and reporter for publications such as *The Wall Street Journal, The Business Journal,* and *The Columbian Missourian*. As a result, he points out, "the only security left is the security you create for yourself."

In addition, says Knowlton, there seems to be an overwhelming desire on the part of increasingly more Americans to fully merge their personal and professional lives. "They believe, as did Thomas Aquinas, that 'to live well is to work well.'"

Take that Job and Love It

Homeworkers embody the real American Dream. Not fame or fortune, but being your own boss. Calling your own shots. Taking control of your life, not necessarily to work more—or less—but to work the way *you* want to work.

These are the people for whom the voice told me to write my book. For them and for the many others soon to join them on their own solitary paths to self-fulfillment.

I didn't want any part of writing this book at first because working alone had long been a bittersweet subject to me. I'd found it tough sledding. I'd often wished for just such a book, one that told me of others with the same emotional obstacles, psychological insecurities, and motivational challenges I faced. And how they solved them. I would have welcomed learning about their struggles and successes, circumventing months and years of painful trial and error.

That's the book the voice told me to write.

"It's probably been done," I countered.

"Find out," the voice persisted.

I finally did.

And the voice was right.

There are books out there on working alone, but they deal mainly with the financial, logistical, administrative, and technological aspects of running a one-person business.

None, I found, focused exclusively on the mental, emotional, psychological, and motivational challenges of surviving on one's own. What goes on *inside* you. The things you have to tell yourself over and over because there's no one else to do it for you. The lessons you have to learn and relearn in your heart and mind. That's the book I knew I wanted to write.

"Why didn't you speak up sooner?" I yelled back. But the voice had finally stopped.

What This Book Will Do for You

On Your Own takes a long, hard, realistic look at the mental, emotional, psychological, and motivational challenges of working alone, and by so doing shows you how to work happily, productively, and successfully from home. What this book doesn't do is trivialize or gloss over the obstacles you may encounter as a solitary worker. It is not another trendy text on the mindless joys of working alone. It *is* a how-to manual, an instruction handbook, a survival guide—for you who are survivors in the truest sense of the word.

This author wholeheartedly endorses M. Scott Peck's fundamental premise that life *is* hard and only gets easier when we learn from the lessons it hands us. Working alone, like life itself, must be mastered in order for the homeworker to be happy, productive, and fulfilled. How does one achieve this? Through discipline.

"Discipline," says Peck, "is the basic set of tools we require to solve life's problems. Without discipline we can solve nothing. With only some discipline we can solve only some problems. With total discipline we can solve all problems."

I certainly applaud the liberated lifestyle millions of Americans have chosen for themselves working alone. Truly these intrepid men and women have achieved the American Dream— the *real* dream, grounded in the primal satisfaction of total self-sufficiency, in the sweet fulfillment of succeeding completely on their own: proud, aloof, serene, free at last from the petty tyrannies and constraints of others.

If you are one of this growing number of fortunate Americans, exult in your magnificent achievement. Cherish your life. *On Your Own* was written for you—to help you live the dream for as long as you want it.

For Those Who Are Struggling

Accept, however, that the downstairs commute may carry a price, that you may encounter problems working where you live, whether alone or with loved ones, and that you must solve these problems in order to succeed as a homeworker. Unfortunately, some people *do* feel isolated working alone. Some people do get lonely. Some people do procrastinate. Some people do lack the self-motivation and self-discipline necessary to succeed by themselves. Some people do struggle to blend home and family with business and work, even though bringing them together is the heart of the dream.

The mental, emotional, and psychological challenges are the reason for this book. It wouldn't exist if I hadn't struggled with them myself.

Life *is* a series of problems, Peck consoles us in his all-time best-selling self-help treasure, *The Road Less Traveled*. And it is this whole process of meeting and solving problems that gives life its meaning. "Problems are the cutting edge that distinguishes between success and failure," Peck assures. "Problems call forth our courage and our wisdom; indeed, they create our courage and our wisdom. It is only because of problems that we grow mentally and spiritually."

Doing It Your Way

Still, each of us must learn in our own way, in our own time, at our own pace. This book, therefore, provides something for everyone. If you're one of those people who'd prefer not to be told how badly something is broke—just how to fix it—there's plenty in here for you, checklists galore. For the more introspective, for those whose solutions must evolve from an understanding of *why* things don't work in the first place, there is a wealth of insight as well.

Here, then, is *On Your Own*, written as much for me as for you, presented with an overriding bit of advice that resounds like a litany throughout its pages:

Keep in mind that these are other people's ways, other people's advice, other people's triumphs. No doubt, you will learn from them. They will guide you, show you the way to your own answers. When you're done reading about these people on their own, you will be grateful for their insights and guidance.

But in the end, you'll find your own way. You'll know what's good for *you*, what's right for *you*. You'll work smarter, quicker, better, happier. You'll be able to count on yourself as never before. Because you'll *know* yourself better than ever.

It's called self-discovery. And it's the greatest gift this book will give you.

For all the courageous wayfarers already on their solitary travels, and for those about to embark, here is an instruction manual, a survival handbook, navigational charts, and a spiritual guide for the journey on the rough but rewarding, turbulent but exciting seas of self-fulfillment.

Sail on, brave voyager.

CHAPTER ONE

AT HOME WITH YOUR JOB: MAKING IT WORK FOR YOU

Home alone, with the job you love.

For millions of Americans, it's the culmination of a lifelong dream. For some, however, it's more like a nightmare. For most, it's inevitably a learning experience—usually a profound one.

"Be careful what you wish for," a wise person once cautioned. "You may get it." Or in Truman Capote's words, "More tears are shed over answered prayers than unanswered ones."

There's a flip side, you see, to each benefit, challenges cordoning every reward, thorns lurking amid the roses, poison ivy bordering primrose paths, rough waters edging smooth sailing. The metaphors are as mixed as the pleasures and perils of being on your own.

WHAT TO EXPECT WHEN YOU GET OFF THE FAST TRACK

Stress and exhaustion are standard tolls on today's corporate roads to success. But getting off the fast track—or even lowering

13

the speed limit—can impose psychological penalties and pressures.

"Warp speed to idle can be tough," cautions Thayer Cheatham Willis, a Portland, Oregon psychotherapist who specializes in treating wealth-related psychological issues. "Peace and quiet, even after relative chaos, can be unsettling when the novelty wears off.

"Like it or not, we are social creatures. What's more, we're pack animals by nature. Human interaction and the feeling of connectedness to others are basic to our sense of self," says Willis.

Some of us, she points out, need more personal contact than others to define ourselves and give meaning to our lives. When social contact is diminished severely, there can be a tendency to fall back on negative behaviors, harmful addictions, and adaptive rituals. One of the latter is overorganization—an endless spinning of wheels before ever getting started.

"Human nature abhors a void," Willis sums up. "We must fill the holes in our lives constructively or they will fill themselves with whatever is most convenient."

Discipline, Determination

Writer Michael Stanton puts it this way: "Free isn't easy. It means risks. It means responsibility. It means hard work. You need discipline to be your own boss, the persistence to follow through in the face of uncertainty and the resilience to overcome the obstacles and rejections."

"You have to understand," points out Misty Kuceris, a television producer/management consultant, "that you're not simply choosing a job, you're choosing a life."

And a lifestyle that isn't for amateurs. Those who think they can fall into it with a minimum of thought, commitment, and effort soon wind up back in the office, murmuring a litany of excuses:

"I began to feel terribly lonely and anxious out there."

"I wound up a much more productive person, but I lost all that schmooze time. I didn't think I'd miss it so much."

"I found I needed to do my business face to face."

"I outgrew my living room. It began to feel like a jail cell."

"I was wearing jeans too often. I needed to reintroduce some tension that would get me to dress up and beat the bushes for new clients."

"I found myself prolonging conversations with phone solicitors and meter readers just to have someone to talk to."

"I couldn't stay out of the kitchen."

"I couldn't stay put. I'd make up excuses to go out, even when I was faced with big deadlines."

"I'd never thought of myself as a procrastinator, but it was becoming my middle name."

"I started to resent my family because I saw them as obstacles to my work—and it showed. My kids were avoiding me. My wife wasn't my biggest fan either."

"I didn't know when to quit working. It seemed I never stopped."

"I thought I knew myself until I started working out of my home."

"I didn't realize how much of my identity I derived from my job."

Work Defines Us

Most of us define ourselves not by who we are but by what we do for a living.

"The work ethic fosters the widely held belief," observes Barbara Brandt of the Shorter Work-Time Group of Boston, "that people's work is their most important activity, and that people who don't work long and hard are lazy, unproductive, and worthless.

"For many Americans today, paid work is not just a way to make money but is a crucial source of their self-worth. Many of us identify ourselves almost entirely by the kind of work we do."

And by how much.

Leisure is certainly a desirable part of his life, Ron Kogen makes clear. But the fun and games have to be planned. They have to be part of the schedule. If they're spontaneous, they make him feel shiftless, "like a wastrel."

Kogen, a doctor of music and a licensed tax consultant, is well aware that his strong work ethic was shaped by his childhood environment. His father was a musician who played his violin on radio shows and spent the rest of his life in his den at home.

"It was his office," says Kogen. "I remember him in there, always busy, happily working away at his desk, composing music, charting stocks, playing chess by mail. When I think of him, that's how I see him—occupied and content.

"It's why I feel I have to be busy and productive to be happy too. I know this now."

The realization has helped Kogan reconcile himself to the lifestyle he knows he must lead to be happy on his own. Although his work is seasonal and compressed into intense periods, he can't kick back and enjoy the slack times, he confesses with a grimace.

Acknowledging Ingrained Traits

We're such a deeply work-oriented society, notes Barbara Brandt, that leisure-time activities such as play, relaxation, cultural and artistic pursuits, quiet contemplation, or just "doing nothing" are regarded as unessential components of life.

Too often held in contempt is the irreverent suggestion that workplaces should nurture employees, and that work can actually be enjoyable and satisfying.

The traditional work ethic of labor for pay and little else is so deeply ingrained in our psyche that society ranks among its most suspect those entrepreneurs, executives, and professionals who allow their hearts to lead their heads; who willingly cut back on their time in the trenches; who choose to work "differently" despite the detrimental effect such heretical actions might have on their earning power.

Something else that used to bother Ron Kogen is what he calls the "image" thing.

"We're so programmed to be conformists," he laments. "It's not easy to break out of the mold. I know it's silly, but there was a time when it was unsettling to me that people were getting up and going to work while I stayed home.

"It made me feel 'unemployed.' I felt *different* shopping at 10 or 11 on a Tuesday morning, when the only others around were housewives and retirees. I finally got over it by telling myself I *was* being silly, but it really bothered me for a while!"

How strongly solitary workers are influenced by the way the world regards them could be a real consideration for certain managers, executives and professionals embarking on their own.

Nonetheless, they are becoming legion, these upstarts who've given themselves a "mulligan" on the back nine of their lives.

THE UPSIDE AND FLIPSIDE OF BEING ON YOUR OWN

What's Great	*What Isn't*
Being your own boss—the greatest job in the world.	Being your own boss—the toughest job in the world.
Being the boss.	And secretary, staff, and janitor as well.
No one telling you what to do.	No one telling you what to do.
Greeting your children at the door.	Greeting your children when you're on deadline.
More time with the family.	Too much time with the family.
Taking the dog for a walk whenever you want.	Having to walk the dog.
Being able to sleep in.	Sleeping too much.
Taking a nap whenever you want.	Not being able to sleep at night.
No more long commutes.	No place to go after work.
No more office politics, squabbling, and socializing.	No one around.
Not having to go out to eat.	Being too close to food.
Being able to work day and night.	Becoming a workaholic.
No dress code.	Becoming a slob.
No more phones ringing incessantly.	Wishing someone would call.
An end to constant interruptions.	No interruptions.

WHAT'S GREAT	WHAT ISN'T
No more expense reports to fill out.	No expense account.
Playing golf on Friday because you can make up your work on Sunday.	Playing golf on Sunday too.
Seclusion.	Isolation.
Solitude.	Loneliness.

BALANCING OPPOSING FORCES

"People who spend a great deal of time by themselves," says psychotherapist Willis, "must be aware of the opposing human drives for love and companionship, on the one hand, and autonomy, individuality and independence, on the other.

"Achieving a healthy balance between these conflicting needs is a challenge for everyone who chooses to work alone."

Those who possess superior creative talent have another isolation factor to contend with. They are often regarded with envy and awe because of their gifts, observes Anthony Storr, internationally acclaimed author of *The Art of Psychotherapy* and *The Essential Jung*. They tend to be thought of as peculiar, he notes, "odd human beings who do not share the pains and pleasures of the average person."

"Does this difference from the average imply abnormality in the sense of psychotherapy?" Storr asks. "More particularly, is the predilection of the creative person for solitude evidence of some inability to make close relationships?"

He answers these questions in his marvelous book, *Solitude: A Return to the Self*:

> The creative person is constantly seeking to discover himself, to remodel his own identity and to find meaning in the universe through which he creates. He finds this a valuable integrating process which, like meditation or prayer, has little to do with other people, but which has its own separate

validity. His most significant moments are those in which he attains some new insight, or makes some new discovery; and these moments are chiefly, if not invariably, those in which he is alone. . . .Perhaps the need of the creative person for solitude, and his preoccupation with internal processes of integration, can reveal something about the needs of the less gifted, more ordinary human being . . .

IS BEING ON YOUR OWN RIGHT FOR YOU?

Now a quiz.

Take it before you move on. Do the exercise without undue circumspection; respond quickly and candidly. You'll score yourself later. The grade will reveal your potential to work successfully on your own.

Assign a score of 1 through 5 to each statement, 1 being the measure of your most negative feelings on the self-assessments below ("You've got to be kidding!"), 5 indicating your most passionate affirmation ("That's me all over!"). In short, a 5 indicates your wholehearted agreement; 1 means it couldn't be further off the mark, as far as you're concerned.

A Self-Assessment Test for Working Alone

1. It's important for me to see tasks through from beginning to end without input or interference from others. ( )

2. When it comes to influencing clients, I think the way I come across is much more critical than my surroundings. ( )

3. I remain motivated in what I'm doing without the encouragement and support of others. ( )

4. Despite little or no outside direction, I seldom have trouble finishing projects. ( )

5. I rarely consult fashion magazines before buying clothes. ( )

6. I don't place much importance on the car I drive. ( )

7. My friends are from diverse lifestyles and professions. ( )

8. I'm seldom influenced by critical comments about my personal appearance or possessions.

9. I'm a risk-taker. ( )

10. I've never considered myself a "team player." ( )

11. When I'm alone, I'm seldom lonely. ( )

12. I tend to underdress more often than I overdress for social occasions. ( )

13. I'm not a boring person. ( )

14. I consider myself a "survivor." ( )

15. I've never had the stomach for office politics. ( )

16. I seldom worry about what people think of me. ( )

17. I think romance and passion are important to personal relationships. ( )

18. I tend to question authority. ( )

19. I usually feel guilty when I'm not working. ( )

20. I regard myself as a perfectionist. ( )

21. I could work much harder than I do. ( )

22. My work is my greatest source of pleasure. ( )

23. I consider myself a nontraditional individual. ( )

24. I usually make up my mind quickly. ( )

25. I don't often consult a lot of people before making important decisions. ( )

26. When others consult me for advice, I tend to offer a lot of options. ( )

27. I usually look forward to starting work each morning. ( )

28. I enjoy solitude. ( )

29. I feel different from most of my co-workers. ( )

30. I hate business meetings. ( )
31. How I feel about myself is more important than what other people think about me. ( )
32. I consider myself a creative individual. ( )
33. I generally adhere to the rule, "Business before pleasure." ( )
34. I enjoy breaking the rules. ( )
35. Daydreaming is an important part of my problem solving, and I often get my best ideas when I'm not doing anything in particular. ( )
36. I'm usually receptive to offbeat, so-called "crackpot" ideas. ( )
37. I tend not to tolerate fools well. ( )
38. I'm sometimes considered a "cold fish." ( )
39. I regard myself as "driven" in my work. ( )
40. I need to control the things I create and for which I'm responsible. ( )

And a final question, not for grading but for you to consider honestly: Am I running toward something? Or just running away? Now add up your score and see how you did.

Rating Your Score

160–plus: You're an excellent prospect to work alone. Go for it!

100 to 159: You're a good candidate, but you've got some work cut out for you.

61 to 99: It'll be tough!

60 or less: I'd think about it some more. A lot more.

Making the Grade

If you scored well on the test, here's what your high mark tells you:

- You're self-confident, self-motivated, self-disciplined, a self-starter.

- You're multifaceted, creative, and flexible. At the same time, you're extremely demanding of yourself and others. People think you have unreasonably high standards, and you agree.

- You're an independent thinker, assertive, decisive, results-oriented, and willing to take risks.

- You dislike regimentation, rigidity, overdirection. In fact, you tend to chafe under any supervision at all.

- You're a tough negotiator, a formidable business opponent.

- It's important for you to control your work. And your life.

- You relish solitude. You're most in tune with yourself when there's no one else around. You actually enjoy your own company. Your greatest insights, finest achievements, and most significant moments come when you're alone.

- You're on your own because you want to be—more than that, because you *have* to be. Because your freedom, independence, and self-reliance are all-important to you.

WHAT IT TAKES TO BE ON YOUR OWN

What does it take to work happily, productively, and successfully on your own? Professional organizer Sue Hurlbut, president of HTO Enterprises, provides a few tips:

GET TO KNOW YOURSELF. Know what's important to your happiness and well-being. Understanding exactly what you're after prepares you to achieve it.

Learn your strengths and weaknesses, then adjust your ego to balance them. You need enough chutzpah to take the emotional and financial risks necessary to succeed on your own. At the same time, however, make sure you don't wield your confidence and self-belief beyond prudence, to the point where your strengths become weaknesses.

Tame your ego enough to seek help, support, and personal growth whether you think you need it or not. Remember, you're your own best friend and your own worst enemy. We need others to help us keep our perspective in the world beyond our office at home.

Be willing to change. Don't be so rigid, bull-headed, or self-centered that you're unable to learn, change, or adapt. Be willing to extend yourself, to stretch emotionally, intellectually, creatively—in every way you can think of.

Be successful every day. Be familiar with the scale on which you measure success so you know how much of it gives you a sense of accomplishment. It's important to feel successful every day. If it takes considerable success to tip your particular scale, you may become discouraged early on.

By reducing the amount of success you need to feel good about yourself, you can maintain your positive energy and momentum.

Open up. Because you enclose yourself in an office, it's important to keep your mind open to new possibilities and your emotional self accessible to new kinds of relationships.

Learn to reach out. Many people learn the hard way that they can't do it all by themselves; they have to ask for help. But even when you *can* do it by yourself, it's more energizing to bring others into the process, to share your successes.

Don't worry, be happy. Like stress, a certain amount of worry is natural and even healthy, but know when to stop. Don't waste your psychic energy on things you can't control.

"Think about what's making you anxious," advises psychologist Elwood Robinson, an associate professor at North Carolina Central University, "then estimate the likelihood that it will happen. If the chances are low, as is often the case, remind yourself of that each time the fear surfaces."

If you do worry, counsels Pennsylvania State University psychologist Tom Borkovec, give yourself permission to do so, but only for a limited period of time—say, for the next 10 minutes. Also confine your worrying to a specific place, suggests Borkovec, who is recognized as the nation's leading authority on worry. If you find yourself fretting at an undesignated time, stop by reminding yourself you'll get a chance to worry later.

HAVE FUN. Joy is an important part of each day. Create as many opportunities for laughter as you can, even if they come at your own expense. The healthiest people in the world are those who can laugh at themselves, and others love them for it.

Remember, a hearty laugh can cure almost everything. Prescribe it for yourself in large, regular doses.

As Mary Pettibone Poole puts it, "He who laughs, lasts."

CHAPTER TWO

TUNING YOUR

PSYCHIC ENGINE:

BEING YOUR

OWN MECHANIC

Think of yourself as an automobile. The car you drive will do: An interdependent assembly of cams, gears, disks, valves, shafts, belts, bearings, flywheels, manifolds, pistons, connecting rods, and more, requiring the right fuel, periodic oil changes, lube jobs, tune-ups, engine overhauls, and replacement parts.

That's a fair description of each of us as well.

Not a collection of chrome, glass, rubber, and steel, but an infinitely more complex commingling of organs, nerves, glands, tissues, veins, muscles, blood, and bones, held together by cartilage, skin, and hair, propelled by intellect, instinct and emotion, composing an organism so responsive as to be miraculous, yet subject to constant breakdown and endless repair.

Keeping your psychic engine running at peak efficiency is a main concern when you work alone because there's no one to do it for you. No pit crews to get you going again when you sputter to a stop.

WHAT MAKES YOU TICK?

It's up to you then, to understand the unique sum of your esoteric parts. What makes *you* stop and start, hum and accelerate, soar and glide? What kind of fuel gives you the best mileage and performance? What gear gets you up the hill fastest? Are you equipped with four-wheel drive or should you steer clear of certain terrain? What emergency repairs do you require? When are you due for your next inspection? What happens to your engine when you miss a tune-up?

In human terms, what motivates you, makes you mentally strong and emotionally secure, maximizes your performance, provides you joy and fulfillment, uplifts and restores you, keeps you on an even track, and gets you to where you're going?

What makes *you* tick?

For human machinery, there are no assembly-line answers.

You have to write your own operator's manual, be your own mechanic, keep your own maintenance chart, craft your own repair tools.

And only by knowing yourself fully will you be able to "fix yourself" to achieve your personal and professional potential.

Most important, then, to people on their own is *self-discovery*. It is their key to survival and success.

In the words of Chinese philosopher Lao-Tzu, "He who knows others is wise; he who knows himself is enlightened." Those on their own need as much enlightenment as they can get: The only answers that count *are* their own.

That's the main purpose of this book—to help you find your answers.

Exceptions Make the Rule

In these pages you'll read about guidelines, best and worst scenarios, DOs and DON'Ts, right ways and wrong ways. Keep firmly in mind, however, that what is generally good may not *always* be good, as far as you're concerned.

There are no absolutes, not for any of us.

Conversely, there is usually something that applies to everyone.

And count on this: There really *is* an exception to every rule, and probably more than one. You learned the lesson as a child: "Jack Sprat could eat no fat, his wife could eat no lean. . ."

So if the first commandment of being on your own is "Whatever works for *you*," ask yourself constantly: "Am I the exception? Or the rule?"

Keep that primary commandment in the foyer of your mind as you open the door to each solution that appears contradictory. It won't seem that way if you remind yourself that no single answer fits everyone. Ask yourself: Does it suit *me*?

Later on, for example, you'll read that good grooming and appropriate attire play a real part in the business success of solitary workers. Because being neat, clean, and properly dressed strongly affects our self-image, especially when no one else is around to influence what we think of ourselves.

Sound advice, you agree.

But then you read about others going from their beds to their computers in their pajamas. They do it purposefully, it is explained, to get a fast start, to stay habitually clear of procrastination's gummy reach.

That's well and good, too, because the tactic works for those individuals, which is all that matters.

Pick Your Style

"The worker from home is similar to any client who comes to my office seeking answers," points out psychotherapist Patricia Megan Pingree. "There are general theories and principles that apply to all, but specific solutions vary from person to person.

"We all need to find the right balance between time spent by ourselves and time spent with others. Only *you* know what mix is right for you," emphasizes Pingree, a licensed professional counselor who specializes in guided imagery techniques.

Whether you work alone by choice or circumstance, she counsels, it is relevant and beneficial to remind yourself often that the greatest benefit of working alone is no longer having to fit your mode of operation to the approval of others. You're finally free to pursue your own goals and desires, to indulge in your own lifestyle, to live up to your own expectations—not anyone else's. What more could you ask?

Lift the Hood

Asked for her advice to solitary motorists on the highway of life, Pingree replies, "Lift the hood once in awhile."

Find out what's going on under there, she urges, especially if you hear a few squeals or knocks. If you don't, it's like seeing the red light on the dashboard go on or the gas gauge hit empty and just driving on, hoping that if you ignore it, it will go away. It won't, of course. It's just another case of "Pay me now or pay me much more later."

"If you find your engine is running rough," Pingree continues, "try to discover where the problem lies—exactly what part of the system needs attention. Determine if repairs are immediate, long-term, or both. If the brakes squeal or the engine won't turn over, rotating the tires won't help. But installing new brake pads or replacing the ignition coil might be just the ticket.

"As a worker from home, if loneliness is bothering you to the point of distraction or you're so disorganized you can't meet your deadlines, don't spend your time shopping for a better computer, at least not yet. Identify what's breaking down and fix it.

"But you can't do so without knowing how your psychic machinery works in the first place—the signals it sends out when a certain part of the system needs attention. You have to be able to read the warning signals and know how to respond properly."

Preventive Maintenance

Psychologist Frank Colistro warms quickly to the analogy of automotive and psychic engines. He owns a 1972 Fiat Spider, he reveals proudly, which he bought brand new and has preserved in mint condition.

"Whether human beings or cars are involved, the key to longevity and peak performance is preventive maintenance," asserts Colistro, who specializes in helping disaffected executives and professionals redefine their business careers and lifestyles. The majority of his clients, he says, work alone.

Even if you know your engine intimately, don't become "error activated," he urges. "Don't wait for a warning signal to alert you to fix something that wouldn't have gone wrong if you'd performed routine maintenance in the first place.

"The old saying, 'If it ain't broke, don't fix, it' doesn't apply here. By the time the red light goes on, 80 percent of the damage has already been done."

HOW TO KEEP YOUR PSYCHIC ENGINE RUNNING SMOOTHLY

Know your trouble spots. Be aware of which areas of your psyche need close attention, constant monitoring, regular overhauls. Be alert to danger signs that signal impending malfunctions. As a worker from home, are you aware when you're procrastinating, for instance? Do you know what to do about it?

Do you have a survival plan for emotional, psychological, and motivational breakdowns? Do you lift your psychic hood regularly? Or just when you *have* to—say, after you limp to a halt on the freeway of life? Do you know exactly what you're looking for when you expose your engine? If not, how are you going to fix anything?

HAVE THE PROPER TOOLS TO BE YOUR OWN MECHANIC. Frank Colistro suggests: the *Three-Question Rule*. Apply it when anxiety strikes—when you become distracted, agitated, mentally fatigued, depressed, or worried.

Keep in mind, says Colistro, that *all anxiety is caused by thought, which, in turn, creates emotion.* Identify the emotion by isolating the thought so you can act on your anxiety or forget about it.

Identify what is bothering you by isolating the thought—say, that you're feeling isolated because you haven't had any human contact for a week. Or you think you didn't ask enough for the job you're doing. Or you're convinced you need a fax machine and modem but you can't afford to purchase them right now. Ask yourself:

1. *Is the thought true?* Am I really lonely? Will I actually not get paid enough for the project? Do I really have to buy that equipment immediately?

2. *Is the thought timely?* Do I have to deal with the problem right away? Can it wait till next week? Next month? Till I've finished this assignment?

3. *Is the thought helpful?* Is it motivating me toward something constructive that should be done immediately? Should I act *now*?

If all the answers are *yes*, then go! Get started on resolving your problem.

If one, two, or all three of your answers are *no*, get back to work! You either don't have a problem or you don't have to solve it right away. The objective, he says, is to stop obsessing over things you can't confront or aren't ready to address immediately. Colistro has even suggested to a client that he put a rubber band on his wrist to zap himself each time he worried needlessly. It worked.

CONSIDER YOURSELF A '61 CORVETTE. Or a classic Mercedes. Not an old junker you don't value too much. Pamper yourself as if you were priceless, which, of course, you are—or should be. Get that lube job and oil change regularly to keep your friction points from overheating. Pull off the road once in a while to let your engine cool down.

Take a full hour for lunch. Exercise regularly. Go on vacation—every year, not every decade. Plan to be on the road a long, long time, purring smoothly, with your chasis and original equipment intact and in good repair.

It's difficult for independent contractors, who operate on the feast-or-famine principle, to refuse a lucrative contract. But we must, when necessary, to pace ourselves for the long haul.

Don't work yourself to a point of physical or emotional exhaustion and have to drop out of the race. Unremitting toil may reap big rewards, but it can also lead to major breakdowns.

Know and value your psychic engine. Understand how it works. Treat it with consideration and respect.

VARY YOUR SPEED. As car enthusiasts well know, engines tend to run better and last longer if the speeds at which they are operated vary. Constant loading tends to wear certain parts excessively. Instead of traveling at a steady 65 miles-per-hour for six straight hours, move your speed around, with an occasional rest stop.

A steady speed is a good rule-of-thumb, but intentionally vary your pace. Put in a 12-hour day at full speed, then kick back to a four- or six-hour day. The variety enhances your engine's flexibility and avoids undue strain on critical parts.

PRACTICE PREVENTIVE MAINTENANCE. Don't become "error activated." Switch to a preventive maintenance system. Don't wait for the warning lights to go on before implementing corrective action. By then, severe physical and psychic damage may have been done that could prove costly to repair.

PICK YOUR BEST ROUTE FOR EACH DESTINATION. Know where you're going at all times and the best ways to get there. Study your road map before each critical journey. Choose the course that's easiest on your psychic engine, and have an alternate route in case of an emergency. Do you know all the detours? Are you aware of any new freeways that've opened up since you last headed in that direction? Do you orient yourself before each trip? Or do you wind up driving around in circles?

WHAT'S IMPORTANT TO YOU: YOUR PERSONAL PIE CHART

This chapter is about deciding what's important to you—using your personal values as a vehicle for achieving your personal and professional goals. Here's an exercise to help you clarify those values in your mind.

Try serving up your personal values in a pie chart. Decide how large a segment you'd allocate to each value. Redo the pie chart every so often. Our values change with time and altered circumstances. So our allocation of time to specific goals should change as well.

Here's a partial list of personal values to get you started. Substitute your own if you like, but include only those that are of paramount importance to you:

- Career
- Family
- Health
- Marriage
- Financial security
- Community involvement
- Spirituality
- Physical appearance

Remember that your goals should have their basis in a value system such as this one. The time and effort you spend pursuing each goal should be proportionate to the importance you assign to it. If so, your life is probably in balance. But only you know for sure.

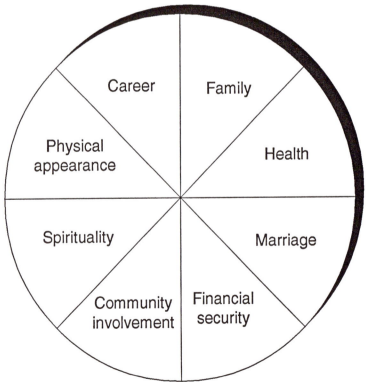

CHAPTER THREE

GETTING

A FAST START:

OUTRACING MENTAL

ROADBLOCKS

Carrying over the analogy of engines, let's talk about turning on the ignition and roaring off each day: Starting with a bang and accelerating out of the reach of mental and emotional paralysis before it creeps up and immobilizes you.

"The idea," says Bernard Malamud, "is to get the pencil moving quickly."

The best way not to let your psychic pipes clog in the first place is to become proficient at the fast start.

Avoid procrastination by cutting right to the chase.

Blast off. Burn rubber. Leave your adversary in the dust.

When Jeff Crawford's not on the road, he cuts to the chase. And he means right *to* it, says the Los Angeles travel writer. Rising promptly at 6 A.M., Crawford makes a beeline from his bed to his computer.

"My first conscious act each working day," he says, "is to boot up the Mac and immediately retrieve whatever document I'm working on. I get it on the screen while I'm still wiping the sleep from my eyes."

The objective, Crawford explains, is to get himself hooked before he does anything else. Only when he's fully caught up in his work does he break off to attend to the more mundane chores of shaving, showering, dressing, and eating. For him, they are secondary considerations. The first order of the day, every day, is to become totally immersed in his job.

He likens this deliberate, immediate involvement to a cork flung into a current. "Once I'm in," he says, "nothing can stop me."

Jump Right In

Marketing consultant Joe Fernandez feels the same way. An early riser, he used to start his morning like most other working people, by bathing, dressing, having breakfast, and reading the morning paper. Then a funny thing happened to him on the way to his basement office.

He began getting an anticlimactic feeling, as if the day was closer to ending than beginning, as if he'd put forth his best effort—used up most of his energy—getting *ready* for work. Now, like Crawford, Fernandez wades right in.

He does it in a calculated effort to get swept up in the business at hand, to expend his mental and physical vigor on the important pursuits of the day.

"I finally figured out that my prime time is the five or six hours after I wake up," he says. "I decided not to waste a minute of that peak energy—to plunge into my work. Now I get right to the important stuff. I shower and dress later, when my concentration and momentum have waned."

Fernandez laughs. "A good day is when I find myself still in my pajamas at two in the afternoon. Then I know I've gotten some real work done."

Crawford and Fernandez are obvious exceptions to the rule that one should prepare suitably for the day's work. They do what they do deliberately because it works for them.

Pick Up Where You Left Off: Make the Most of Yesterday's Energy

Plunging into the workstream is easier if you don't do it cold turkey by tackling something brand new right off. Getting started is half of most battles, and the toughest half at that. So make it easy to get going. Once you're off the starting blocks, adrenaline takes over. The rest is cruise-control.

The trick is to launch yourself each morning with energy left over from the day before. And to leave the trampoline up, so to speak, so that when you leap into your work, you're catapulted right back up.

A ploy I use on myself is to leave the chapter, the page, the paragraph, even the sentence I'm working on unfinished—hanging there for me to grab, like Tarzan, for a swinging start the next morning. I do the same whenever I take a break.

A favorite place for me to quit is in the middle of transcribing a quote so I don't have to dredge up any creative energy when I begin again. Or I start by editing what I wrote the day before. Or by simply retyping a paragraph or two, even a page. It gets me back in the game quickly.

Again, observe your own natural tendencies. Ask yourself: Will suspending work at the psychological crest of my psychic energy make it easier for me to recapture my momentum when it's time to start again? If not, you may as well ride out that momentum and apply the brakes when you drift into the trough of the work wave. In short, adjust your daily routine and activities to the incoming and outgoing tides of your mental, emotional, and physical energy.

HOW TO OUTFOX YOUR INERTIA

Kick-starting an engine is much easier on the decline of a hill. If I know I'll need a push in the morning, why park on an incline? For me, the danger in getting restarted when a new or tedious task is facing me is that I'll put it off because it requires too much of an effort to get going. That's procrastination: Putting things off.

Put yourself in motion instead. Generate your own velocity instead of waiting for the spirit to move you. Make it easy to get rolling by leading off with a familiar rather than unknown project. Start with something interesting, not boring or intimidating.

Save the taller hurdles for later, when you've achieved some momentum, when it's easier to shift into high gear. The hills are easier to take that way. And it's easier on the engine.

"If you're energized by having a great idea, put a creative project at the head of the list," suggests Sue Hurlbut, a professional organizer and producer of audiovisual products on productivity training.

If talking with others about what you're doing revs your engine, get on the phone, she says. Or schedule regular breakfast meetings.

If landing a sale lights your fire, dive into the day by phoning your hottest prospects.

"If having the phone ring gets you pumped, make sure it happens," Hurlbut adds. "Encourage people to call you early. Tell them you're most accessible then."

Figure a way to jump-start yourself every morning, and the trip will be a Sunday drive.

Reward Yourself: Dangle a Carrot

Dangle an incentive in front of your nose if that's what it takes to get going.

Are you a coffee lover? Put off that first tempting cup until you're well into your first hour of work. Or until you've met a personal goal.

Are you a crossword nut like travel agent Jim Hertz? ("Give me *The New York Sunday Times* puzzle and you've lost me for half the morning," he says ruefully.) If so, promise yourself a puzzle. Or a chapter from the novel you're reading. Or a brisk walk. Or a therapeutic hour in the garden. Or a latte at the espresso shop down the street. Whatever pushes your motivational button.

But *after* you've earned it.

Put the chore *before* the carrot, the labor before the reward.

"Any discipline or indulgence that actually helps nudge you into position is acceptable and productive," encourages novelist/writing instructor Janet Burroway.

"If jogging after breakfast energizes your mind, then jog before you sit. If you have to pull an all-nighter on a coffee binge, do that. If you have to be chained to your chair, invest in a chain," urges Burroway.

Program Your Starts:
Pavlovian Responses to Start Your Day

Working from Home authors Paul and Sarah Edwards advise imposing rituals on yourself to get moving at appointed times.

If, for instance, you work on the West Coast, you might start the day by calling people in other time zones while the discounted long-distance rates are in effect: Before people break for lunch, for example, or leave their offices for home. The time differences impose rigid deadlines for getting things done.

Be aware of how much your phone rates increase with the passing minutes. Escalating long-distance costs present a natural spur to action. Your long-distance operator can tell you exactly how much phone calls cost at different times of the day or night.

That should be enough of an incentive for homeworkers on Pacific Standard Time to get their show on the road early.

If you customarily see clients, schedule your first appointment for the beginning of the day, suggest the Edwards. "You can also start work when you hear the closing music of a morning news show, watch children leave for school or a spouse for work, or after exercise."

Think of yourself as Pavlov's dog responding to something, anything, that starts the juices flowing, puts you in motion, and gets the day under way.

Consumer behavior analyst Lin Stockton gets up at 7:00 A.M., showers and dresses for work, steps into her car at exactly 7:45, drives eight blocks to a convenience store, buys a large container of coffee, drives back to the office in her three-bedroom townhouse, and drinks the coffee at her desk while she reads the morning paper. When the coffee is gone, she promptly starts work.

The coffee she buys isn't as good as she could brew in her own kitchen in a fraction of the time, concedes Stockton. But that's inconsequential. What's important, she stresses, is her daily ritual, the ceremonial call to action she formally repeats each working day to get herself going.

A similar ritual does the job for investment counselor Dick Chan. He drives to a nearby cafe for coffee and two slices of unbuttered whole wheat toast, then drives home again and goes to work.

"It starts my day," Chan says simply.

Launch your day in your own way, but do it deliberately, consciously, ceremoniously. As Lin Stockton puts it, "It ain't crazy if it works." But it's smart.

EIGHT WAYS TO GET UNDER WAY QUICKLY

Here are some rituals for getting the day started fast. Pick one. Or come up with your own.

1. *Set an alarm.* This is so obvious. Few people do it, but it's effective. Set an alarm clock, a really loud one, without a snooze button. Put it in the living room or kitchen. If an alarm propels you out of bed in the morning, why not use it to spur yourself into action? When it goes off, get into that office and start working! No postponements or delays.

2. *Make an early appointment.* Schedule a 7 or 8 o'clock breakfast meeting, work session, or client visit. Anything to get you up and about.

3. *Join the dawn patrol.* Be an early bird at your health club. Start the day with a workout before heading to the office. Just make sure the workouts launch you into productivity. If they have an opposite draining effect, exercise in the middle or at the end of your day.

4. *Post a reward.* If you feel yourself wavering when it's time to get started, get off the mark by promising yourself a treat when your work is done. Set a quota for yourself and collect a reward when you meet it. Start early, work hard, and get done so you can enjoy the fruits of your labor. Turn on that afternoon game on TV. See a matinee movie. Catch an early aerobics class. Go for a bike ride. Take a hike. Or a siesta.

5. *Have a clear signal for starting.* Like a boxer answering the bell, swing into action at a preordained signal. Be primed to respond to a clear, undeniable call to arms. React to the stimulus automatically, without question or delay. Pick your own energizer: The eighth chime of the grandfather clock, the end of the morning

news show you usually watch, the sound of your neighbor's car pulling out of the driveway, the last gulp of your second cup of coffee.

Let whatever signal you choose galvanize you into action.

6. *Use synchronicity.* Webster's defines the word "synchronous" as "recurring or operating at exactly the same periods." It means to start with one conscious act that leads to another, then another, and another in a tightly knit pattern that eventually takes you exactly where you want to be.

Beth Chadwick, for example, rises promptly at 6 A.M. to let her golden retriever out of the house. From the front door, she heads straight to the bathroom for a shower. Immediately after getting dressed, she brews two cups of coffee, which she leisurely consumes while reading the morning paper. The last sip of her morning coffee takes her back to the front door to let in her dog. From there, Chadwick and her pet proceed directly to a basement office where she commences her day as a payroll consultant.

Most of us are synchronous in our daily activities simply because we tend to be creatures of habit. It's a good thing, however, to use synchronicity deliberately, mindlessly, automatically, in getting a fast start in our daily work. Tie one activity firmly to another, and to another, and another, so that the first move leads you inexorably to a second and a third and a fourth action until you wind up where you want to be—in your office, on time, commencing your work.

7. *Follow a regular routine.* Familiarity may breed contempt in some circles, but for people on their own it fosters a measure of contentment. Try to be consistent in your work habits. Settle into a familiar routine as to when and where you pursue your livelihood at home. In so doing, you are consciously and subconsciously accepting, even welcoming, the daily activity. What's more, you're mentally gearing up for it each morning. A comfortable routine makes fast starts that much easier.

8. *Start with the things you enjoy.* To slip into her work flow quickly, Joleen Colombo does what she enjoys most *first.* "I start with the pleasurable tasks on my daily agenda—the ones that

energize me," she says. "Returning phone calls usually tops the list."

It's important that she be in fourth gear soon after cruising into her office on the top floor of her triplex apartment because that's where she tackles her second job—usually after arriving home spent from her first job. By day Colombo is a public relations coordinator for a public housing authority; evenings and weekends she edits a literary magazine she owns with three other partners. So getting a fast start the second time around is critical to her.

There's a down side, however, to taking care of all the fun stuff first. It leaves her with all the tasks she'd rather avoid, and the longer they remain undone, the larger they loom in her mind. Then they start to weigh her down, she says, and she gets depressed, so it's essential that she dispose of these chores as well. Colombo does it in the same way she orders from a Chinese restaurant menu: Two from Row "A," three from Row "B." Mix and match. It usually works, she says.

CHAPTER FOUR

BUILDING
SELF-DISCIPLINE,
MOTIVATION,
EMOTIONAL TENACITY

Most Americans work harnessed to others, commuting daily to the nation's commercial and industrial beehives. It's become the way of the world, what the majority of us are used to doing. And the truth is, most people need a firm guiding hand. But it's infinitely tougher when that hand is our own because we've become used to the guiding hands of others.

What's critical to solitary workers, then, is what happens to us when the bridles and reins come off. When we're on our own, left to our own devices.

To our self-discipline.

A fortunate few have more of it than they need. Most of us can use as much as we can get.

SELF-DISCIPLINE:
VITAL AS AIR WHEN YOU'RE ON YOUR OWN

George Washington called it the "soul" of an army. "It makes small numbers formidable," he said, "procures success to the weak and esteem to all."

41

The father of our country was talking about discipline, that critical attribute all armies, corporations, organizations, and individuals must possess in abundance. This essential commodity is even more precious to solitary workers because each of us must come up with our own supply—which makes it *self*-discipline and that much harder to attain.

Add the fact that the toughest job in the world is being your own boss. The hardest person to command is yourself, which leads to the pivotal question: "Am I strong enough to do it?"

Catering to another's wishes may not always be pleasant, but it's usually easier than bending to our own not-so-inflexible will. That's what each of us must learn: To carry through on our own. To become our own iron taskmasters. Hard. Uncompromising. Ruthless, if necessary.

Self-discipline, therefore, is as essential to being our own boss as the air we breathe.

KNOW YOURSELF: HOW MUCH SELF-MOTIVATION DO YOU REQUIRE?

As home workers, we must be able to generate our own supply of discipline, the way our lungs work instinctively to provide enough oxygen to keep us alive. Some of us require more oxygen than others—it's a matter of lung capacity. And some of us need more self-motivation and discipline to succeed on our own; like physical stamina, it's a matter of previous conditioning.

What's critical, therefore, is to determine how much self-control you need. Must you keep yourself on a short leash or can you allow yourself a longer lead?

Beyond keeping yourself in check—mixing a few more metaphors—what kind of fuel keeps you operating at peak efficiency, gets your engine racing at full bore? What octane rating gives you the most mileage per tankful? (Instead of *gas*, read *self-motivation*.)

That's what the following pages are about: Generating and maintaining whatever self-motivation and discipline you need to achieve your full potential.

Former Marine Tells How

Gene McLemore is one of those enviable people who has enough self-discipline to pass around. Little wonder, though, as he went through three boot camps: The U. S. Army's, the U. S. Marine Corps', and finally West Point's "beast barracks" for plebes upon his appointment to the U. S. Military Academy. Following five years of active service, including a year in Vietnam, McLemore embarked on a sales career with Xerox, Honeywell, McDonnell Douglas Corporation, and QTC, a small software company.

Happily retired at the tender age of 55 ("unless something short-term comes along") and waiting for his schoolteacher wife, Jean, to do the same, McLemore reflects on a lifetime of working alone. "I was always in a remote office—on my own most of the time," he says. "And I loved it."

What did he learn worth passing along?

KEEP ON TRUCKIN'. As motivated as he was, confesses McLemore, there were times when he just didn't want to get out of bed—when he dreaded the day's activities. He laughs. "Long before Nike adopted the slogan, I just *did* it. It's the best advice in the world."

He always scheduled breakfast rather than luncheon meetings, he says. "Get 'em at breakfast," he'd tell himself, "and the things they take to the office will be yours."

Meeting someone for breakfast would also propel him into full stride early. In that way, he couldn't tell himself that since he was meeting a client for lunch, he didn't have anything to do until then. It forced him to put in a full day.

To "keep things rolling," he'd use his lunch hour to phone his head office.

As for cocktails, they were reserved for the close of day—again, to keep from blunting his momentum. He looked forward to a drink, he says, but at the appropriate time, and for another important reason besides relaxation or the reward for a day well spent.

"For people who work alone," McLemore believes, "the ritual of an evening drink is a good thing. It's a line you cross that clearly marks the end of one thing and the beginning of another. For many, that ritual is the evening commute home. Conversely, the morning compute prepares them for the start of work. People who are already home need a demarcation line to cross, a process that decompresses them for their life after work."

That line could be as simple as turning on the TV set. Or putting on some music. Or changing your clothes, the way you'd get out of your suit as soon as you got home when you used to work downtown. Anything that tells you you're done, through, finished with work for the day.

LEARN TO SAY NO

Like McLemore, journalist Pat McCoy exudes confidence and self-control. Like McLemore, too, she feels she's eminently suited to her solitary vocational lifestyle.

"If anything," says the 48-year-old field reporter for an agricultural newspaper based 450 miles from her Idaho home, "I'm probably overly content being by myself, even though there are times when my territory seems overwhelming and I feel a great deal of pressure."

How does she handle it?

By saying *no*. "It's a keenly important tactic of working alone," she stresses. "I've learned to cry 'Uncle!' when I feel I have to. Not being able to say no can be personally and professionally disastrous when you're on your own."

Time-management and organization experts strongly agree.

"You must avoid getting too many monkeys on your back or risk collapsing from terminal niceness," cautions Dorothy Lemkuhl, author of *The Organizing Bible*.

"Monkeys spring from everywhere—from managers, employers, peers, and yes, even from yourself," she warns.

"People who can't say no to these monkeys—promises, commitments, obligations, overprogramming, impossible personal and professional standards—want to be liked. But ironically, they wind up saying no in a much more disappointing fashion, by getting into trouble and failing to honor everything they've committed to. This failure results in exhaustion, failure, chaos, and guilt," says Lemkuhl. And *more* stress.

"Learn to say no, as often and as adamantly as necessary—to yourself as well as others," she advises.

"Armed with the confidence that you're working on the most important tasks for yourself and your company or clients, learn to control your own destiny by declining nonproductive work. Saying no when it's warranted earns respect—from yourself and from others."

Beware Desire to Belong

Many people on their own find it hard to turn others down, sympathizes organization expert Sue Hurlbut. But it's imperative they learn to do that or risk being swamped with too much to do.

"We who work alone have to be wary of our willingness to substitute *activity* for *productivity*," she explains.

"It stems from our need to be with others, to create acceptance and a sense of belonging in our communities and our civic, professional, and fraternal organizations. This strong desire to belong and to contribute can lead us to become too active on behalf of others.

"While contributions of this sort are commendable and important," she concedes, "we need to guard against overcommitting our time at the expense of the focused productivity our business needs to succeed."

Be clear in your mind about what you can accomplish, and equally clear about what you can't handle. And act accordingly.

FIVE WAYS TO GRACIOUSLY, BUT EFFECTIVELY, SAY "NO!" TO OTHERS

Sue Hurlbut suggests a few ways to say no in a positive manner:

1. *"No, but you might ask. . ."* Whenever possible, when you decline a request for your services, suggest a qualified alternate or two. It's an old story: Those who get things done are the ones who always get asked, even when they're not the best ones for the job. By coming up with someone as capable as you, a candidate who

may be too modest or not as well known, you'll have solved the problem and maybe even provided a better solution.

2. *"No, I really can't take that on right now, but I could on . . ."* Offer an alternative date if you really would like to handle the assignment. The other person's schedule might be adaptable to yours. By making a sincere attempt to accommodate the request, you show your willingness to accept and take the edge off your refusal.

3. *"No, I can't handle all of it, but I'd be willing to do this for you. . ."* Offer to accept whatever part of the project that's agreeable to you. Even suggest that two heads are better than one, that a team can achieve better results with less individual effort. In any case, your honest attempt to help makes your refusal almost all right.

4. *"No, it's really not possible right now, but keep me on the list and I'll do my best to help you out next time."* One of the reasons we say yes when we'd prefer to say no is because, in rejecting the request, we feel we're rejecting the individual who is making it. We feel guilty because we don't like to be rejected ourselves. Assuage your guilt by sincerely asking for a rain check.

5. *"No, I just don't have the time. I really wish I could do this, but I have to be honest with you—it's totally out of the question."* This is a flat-out refusal, but you can soften it by trying to briefly explain why you can't even consider taking on the assignment. Most of us have had the aggravating experience of having someone commit to something and not follow through, regardless of how well-intentioned the person was in accepting in the first place. It's like giving directions to a motorist when you're not quite sure you're right. Your sincere desire to help doesn't justify sending the poor soul off in the wrong direction. Better to say you just don't know.

Hurlbut offers a few last words of advice on learning to say no to others: Put yourself temporarily in their shoes. "If you want to say no and have it accepted graciously," she advises, "be gracious whenever someone says no to you. Be magnanimous, whichever end of the refusal you're on."

OVERCOMING SELF-DOUBT

Walter Scott Gibson knew he had to convince himself he was good enough to succeed on his own before he could convince anyone else. He did it by reaching outside himself.

After 22 years in what he calls "the great black hole of government service," Gibson wanted out. "I was bored stiff," says the 62-year-old former computer programmer/systems analyst. I was part of everything you've ever heard was wrong with working for the government." He dreamed of launching a new career in technical writing.

But first he had to believe in himself, to mute the voices in his head that scoffed at his aspirations: You're just a government hack. You'd be a fraud as a writer. You'd never make it on your own.

Gibson had been a loner all his life, he says, the epitome of the social wallflower: "I was a real shrinking violet, the last to thrust myself forward in pursuit of what I wanted, the least likely to succeed at virtually everything because I was never willing to try. I knew I had to overcome that deadly mindset or remain in my black hole forever."

Gibson climbed out. Thoughtfully, methodically, he extricated himself from debilitating self-doubt, the way all of us who rely solely on ourselves must do.

How to Create Belief in Yourself

He enrolled in courses and workshops on personal development and new careers. He devoured motivational books and tapes. He interviewed successful freelancers he wanted to emulate. He attended self-help courses and seminars.

"One of the classes," Gibson recalls, "was worth the price of admission just to hear someone say, 'We're all much more capable than we think. We only have to believe it.'"

Repeatedly he heard people urge: Get involved! Get off the sidelines and into the game! Just do it! Now! He finally assembled a presentation portfolio, appraised it, and came to the conclusion it was a highly respectable display of work. The prospects he called on agreed. Gibson never looked back.

Today he works from a three-bedroom condo he shares with his wife, Eloise. He had furniture makers come in, he says, and convert their home's smallest bedroom into what he calls his *Better Homes and Gardens* office. It has custom-built cabinetry, shelving, bookcases, and desks, full-spectrum lighting, computer equipment, a laser printer, fax, and phone.

Currently in demand beyond his capacity to accept more work, he has the best of both worlds, he claims, because some clients insist he work from his home while others provide him with an office at their company.

As for his enervating doubts and fears, they're not entirely gone but have receded into the distance. "I've reached a time in my life," he says proudly, "when I can call myself a real success, financially and otherwise. The best part is that I took a huge risk and survived. Without the risk, there's really no achievement."

HOW TO SAY "YES!" TO YOURSELF

Dr. William Zieverink, who served as a staff psychiatrist for the Vietnam Prisoner of War Re-entry Program at Wright Patterson Air Force Base in 1973, offers these words of encouragement and advice to people struggling to make it on their own:

KEEP YOUR MISSION AND GOALS CLEARLY IN MIND. Stay focused on what you're trying to attain. Envision your future clearly. Emotionally experience your life moving forward. Accept as inevitable the successes you will achieve. Know, beyond any doubt, that you will triumph.

BE PASSIONATE ABOUT YOUR WORK. Rekindle the flame daily. Affirm the meaning work has for you in your personal life. Let it center and sustain you. Let it affirm who you are. Let it validate and enrich your existence.

IMPOSE STRUCTURE IN YOUR LIFE. People who work with others have it done for them. As a solitary worker, you have to do it for yourself. We all need a sense of order, restraint, and discipline, some of us more than others.

Medical science once believed, for instance, that most young-sters afflicted with attention deficit hyperactivity disorder (ADHD) simply outgrew the collection of neurological syndromes and behaviors. Not anymore.

Clinical psychologist Lynn Weiss, for one, contends the disor-der is much more prevalent in adults than had been assumed, and that it continues to cause problems into adulthood relating to atten-tion and impulsivity. Adults with the disorder tend to be moody, restless, fidgety, quick-tempered, and appear to possess low-stress tolerance, poor organization, and time-management skills.

Self-help techniques include restructuring and visualization. (Chapter 11 deals entirely with self-affirmation and visual imagery methods.) Suspected sufferers should seek treatment to deal effec-tively with the disorder as it affects their personal and profession-al lives. If you think you need help setting up a working regimen, get it. There are counselors and therapists who specialize in this field.

So be honest with yourself. Assess your true capacity for organization, self-motivation, and self-discipline.

KNOW WHAT DISTRACTS YOU. The best way to avoid "sin," cler-ics advise, is to avoid the occasions of sin. Knowing what weakens your resolve to work or causes your mind to wander will help you steer clear of diversions and stay the course to success.

KNOW THERE WILL BE TIMES OF DOUBT, PANIC, AND FEAR. It's human to experience these emotions, particularly when you want something very badly. Formulate and rehearse your strategies for dealing with such periods of uncertainty. Draw from past success-es to show yourself you can, indeed, cope and triumph. Be ready to reassure and focus yourself when the bad moments come. You really can talk yourself into success! (See Chapter 11.)

Fear of failure is the strongest motivation most people on their own will experience. They know the only thing they can do to avert failure is dig in and work! After enough successes, their motivation takes other forms such as personal satisfaction, self-fulfillment, peer recognition, and financial reward.

But initially it's fear of failure that drives the average home worker. So accept your dread and nausea, and put that energy to work.

REALIZE YOU'RE NOT PERFECT. This is critical to working alone. Recognize your weaknesses as well as your strengths. Acknowledge your limitations so you can compensate for them. Get help from others in areas where you think you need it. You jeopardize your success when you convince yourself you don't need any help, and that you can do it all yourself. No one can. Accept this fact, and it will make you stronger.

WORK ACTIVELY. The more vigorous you are in your work, the better able to concentrate and maintain your focus, the more you'll attain. The process needn't be a sedentary one, whatever your occupation. Who says you have to *sit* there the whole time? You might when you toil with others, but not when you work alone.

Get up and move around. Stick your head out the window and take some deep breaths. Pace the floor. Do some pushups, situps, jumping jacks. Get the adrenaline pumping. Practice a few dance steps. Crank off a set of exercises with your barbells. Just don't get so wrapped up in your energizing diversions that you forget what you're doing, which is working. But work actively, not passively. It will show.

DO SOMETHING CONSTRUCTIVE EVERY DAY. Take a proactive role in pursuing your goals. Regard your progress as inevitable and fully deserved—the result of your irrepressible daily efforts. A feeling of accomplishment and control is basic to your success and extremely effective in overcoming depression. Savor the fruits of your labor, however tiny, every step of the way. It is uplifting to the spirit and propels you forward.

BELIEVE IN YOUR MASTERY OVER YOUR FATE. Realize that a sense of powerlessness defeats you. Survivors truly believe they can effect change, that they can make things happen. Remind yourself: I am not a victim, not a passive recipient of whatever life deals me. I can play the hand. I can influence whatever happens to me because I'm in control. I am an achiever.

Believe it!

One way to convince yourself, suggests PR professional Joleen Colombo, is to deliberately measure your success.

First, define your goal.

Second, create an accurate measure of that goal.

Third, monitor that measure to see if your goal is realistic.

Fourth, celebrate your success.

As an example, Colombo cites, Laura Anderson, a friend in Santa Rosa, California who is a professional caregiver of other people's pets when their owners are on vacation. She contracts to visit her clients' homes while they're away, feed the animals, keep them company a while, walk the dogs, and water the plants.

Worried she might not be able to sustain her home-based business, the pet caretaker set a goal for herself: 30 additional clients within six months. This objective forced her to think of ways to achieve her goal. The measurement was easy. The success when it came was obvious—she suddenly had *too* many clients. All that was left was to celebrate her success—not a disagreeable task at all but a sensible one, says Colombo.

"Always applaud yourself for doing well," she urges. "Rewarding yourself when you deserve it is the lynchpin of self-motivation."

CHAPTER FIVE

DEVELOPING ORGANIZATION SKILLS: MAXIMIZING PRODUCTIVITY

Dana Corwin was about to hit the wall as far as working alone is concerned. The 43-year-old media consultant buys advertising time and space for her clients, a service she performs exceedingly well. But she was starting to feel she'd be better off working for an agency again, even though she could make more money on her own.

Corwin's problem was organization, rather her complete lack of it, working from home.

"This is a deadline business," bemoans the former media director who became a freelancer in 1988. "It requires enormous attention to detail. It demands that I crisply and efficiently clear whatever's on my business plate every working day. There's no room for sloppiness or spillover.

"I knew all that and yet it was a daily struggle to remain disciplined and organized. I was on the edge of chaos, with disaster just around the corner."

Corwin found the paperwork overwhelming. She felt she could barely deal with it. Often she'd have to walk away until she could summon enough strength to face the stacks of paper again. But she knew exactly what she had to do to stay in control. It would have taken just an hour a day, mostly spent sorting her forms and files.

SMALL STEPS THAT LEAD TO BIG ORGANIZATION

But when the time came, she says, she didn't have the energy or inclination to do it. So she operated from moment to moment, letting things fall into greater disarray until she'd have to play massive catch-up, which inevitably exhausted and depressed her. Finally, she decided she had to "drastically clean up my act," Corwin relates.

And she did.

"It's stupid and self-destructive to keep doing things like that," she rebuked herself. "Your mind's a mess because the office is a mess and vice versa. Yet you can't bring yourself to straighten either one out. Instead, you put your energy into emotionally beating yourself up."

Corwin began turning her life around. She quit eating at her desk. She stopped playing video games and writing personal letters on the computer during working hours. She started getting herself organized in dozens of small but important ways such as using a notebook or file form—instead of scraps of paper, bits of envelope, and even dirty napkins—to take down information over the phone.

"I'm O. K. now," she reveals with a sheepish grin. "I just wish I'd never let things get so bad. Letting yourself get disorganized is like being caught in an avalanche. Before you know it, you've been buried alive and swept away."

Organization Is Your Rudder

For home workers everywhere, self-discipline must manifest itself through *organization*. Without it, we are ships without rudders, certain to run aground.

"Good organization is critical to focus and productivity," emphasizes Sue Hurlbut, who installs office systems and trains business clients how to use them efficiently. "Good organization is a flexible framework that accommodates both the routine and the unexpected.

"Good organization accepts change and is capable of stretching and moving in new directions. It allows us to focus our energies by removing road blocks that keep us from performing each task in the most direct, proficient manner. It builds sound habits that streamline the way we get things done."

Yet being organized needn't cramp your spontaneity or dull your creative edge, Hurlbut points out. Furthermore, there's a big difference between being organized and being obsessively neat: "Some people say they can't work in a structured environment, that it takes the flexibility and fun out of life. On the contrary, I think that when you're organized and in control, there's more room for spontaneity and innovation.

"Being well-organized gives you time for other things. That's what organization provides—time for other things."

ORGANIZATION: YOUR PASSPORT TO TIME MANAGEMENT

"Time for other things through organization!" could be John Goveia's motto.

A tenured college professor and practicing CPA with a Ph.D. in economics, Goveia prepares annual tax returns for about 100 clients and serves as a financial consultant for several small businesses in town. In addition, he serves as an expert witness in an average of six court cases a year, presenting financial testimony in support of death and injury claims. He does these extracurricular activities alone, considering them a natural adjunct to his academic duties because they keep him current on tax law and cost accounting, which are the subjects he teaches.

His huge work load notwithstanding, the 44-year-old professor manages to carve out enough leisure time to sail his boat regularly on a nearby river. A physical fitness enthusiast who used to run marathons, he now holds his thrice weekly jogs down to 10 miles an outing but also indulges his passion for hiking, bicycling, tennis, lap-swimming, and cross-country skiing. Despite his crammed schedule, he is rated by his friends as the most laid back person they know.

Asked how he does it, he replies: Organization!

Seven Ways to Keep Organized

Goveia's common-sense advice on "shoehorning" as much as possible into your life:

1. *Continually clear the decks.* Get everything done that you possibly can, without delay, even if it means putting in longer hours before you quit for the day. Don't figure on having enough time tomorrow. In fact, *count* on not having enough time tomorrow, for one simple reason: You probably won't. You don't know what the next phone call or mail delivery is going to bring. If you find you *do* have enough time, and not enough work to fill it, consider it a bonus. Enjoy yourself. You've earned it!

2. *Rely on yourself.* Hope that people will do the things they promise, *when* they promise, but don't bank on it. Accept the fact that most people *will* be late getting you what you need to do the job for them on time. Factor that expectation into all your equations. Compensate for it. Don't ever let it catch you off guard.

3. *Get it done the first time.* Don't duplicate tasks unnecessarily. When someone phones me for material relating to their forthcoming tax return, I get an envelope and write the person's name and address directly on it—not on a piece of paper—so I won't have to transcribe the information onto the envelope later. Then I insert the information into the envelope—while I have the individual's file out—seal the envelope, put a stamp on it, and place it in my "out" box. That way, I'm done with the chore and it's off my mind.

I do most things the first time around.

When I open my mail, I immediately decide whether I'm going to discard, file, or act on each item. Then I *do* it. I don't put anything aside to pick up and consider again later. It's a cliché, but try not to handle any piece of paper more than once. Make a habit of completing every task you start without having to go back to it.

That's efficiency: Doing things with as little waste motion as possible.

4. *Be prepared.* Inefficiency is finishing six tasks when you could have completed 16 or 26. Anticipate what's coming up. Prepare for it. If it doesn't show, you haven't lost anything.

5. *Don't sweat the small stuff.* I used to do it all myself, the big jobs and the little ones, figuring I had to because I was on my own. Now I get others to do some of it for me, on the basis that my time is valuable and I can afford to pay. Not having to do certain work myself is *worth* paying for. For instance, I hire students at an hourly rate to do data input, the way I contract with professionals to paint my house.

As I've gotten busier and more experienced, I've become extremely selective about what warrants my personal attention and what doesn't. I leave the mechanical stuff to others, the way dentists use technicians to clean their patients' teeth.

6. *Get it on paper, or tape.* Don't try to carry everything around in your head. Get it down. I preserve the things I want to remember by jotting notes to myself on those sticky note-pads. Then I put them where I'm sure to see them later—on my phone, in my wallet, on the seat of my chair, by my car keys, on the dashboard of my car.

When I'm home reading or watching TV and I think of something I have to do in the office the next day, I call my work phone immediately and leave a message to myself on my answering machine. Most of the time, two-thirds of the messages on my recorder are from me to myself. By not trusting myself to remember, I make sure I *will* remember by preserving the idea, thought, or scrap of information then and there, while I'm thinking of it.

7. *Stay physically fit.* Exercise is a great way to relieve anxiety, stress, frustration, and daily pressure, as well as to recharge emotional batteries. Take time off to exercise or simply relax, doing whatever you enjoy. Don't consider the time wasted. It pays *huge* dividends.

HOW TO DO MORE WITH LESS EFFORT

Because we're all uniquely different individuals working at myriad jobs, no single organizational system or set of rules suits everyone, says Sue Hurlbut. But there are certain universally applicable principles. She offers some generic tips on working better, quicker, and with less misplaced effort:

Handy Is Dandy

Everything you use in your work should be measured by how often you use it. The items you handle most should be the easiest for you to reach. Keep them *in* or *on* your desk. The items you use less often—but *do* use, say every few weeks—should be kept somewhere in the room or nearby.

As for the things that seldom or never come to mind, store them permanently or discard them. Hanging onto something because there might come a time in your life when you'll need it doesn't make sense. When that time comes, if it ever does, chances are you won't remember the item or where you put it.

Try not to clutter your office, your desk, or your mind. Obstacle courses are cluttered, and deliberately hard to navigate. Airport runways, on the other hand, are spacious and bare—conducive to great take-offs.

If you're like most people, your desk drawers are tiny graveyards, full of little things that serve no functional purpose. When the drawers get full, these useless items pile up, usurping valuable space and creating miniature obstacle courses. Get rid of them!

The average person spends 20 minutes a day just looking for things. That adds up to almost 84 hours a year. At $10 an hour, it comes to $833 of your time. At $20 an hour, that's $1,666! Think about it.

Make Molehills Out of Mountains

Learn to turn each pinnacle you're about to climb into a series of knolls, the way recovering alcoholics handle one day at a time in their lifelong commitment to sobriety.

Organizer Lucy Hedrick likens it to eating an elephant one bite at a time.

Dorothy Lehmkuhl puts it this way: "Success by the yard is hard. Success by the inch is a cinch."

Cut each project down to size by converting it into a sequence of manageable events. Achieve this breakdown by listing all the tasks that compose the project.

Alongside each activity, estimate the amount of time it will take to complete the job. If any of the tasks run longer than 30 minutes, see if they can be broken down further into smaller activities. Try to wind up with chores that can be done in several minutes to no more than half an hour. All that's left is for you to put the series of minor tasks in sequential order. And get started!

So think big—but plan small.

Aim for the horizon, but figure on getting there in short steps.

Create Checklists

Turning mountains into molehills is not only efficient, it can be highly motivating as well. As each "do-able" task on the list is completed and checked off, your feeling of accomplishment will heighten along with your sense of being in charge of the project—not vice versa, as it often seems with people not in total control of what they're doing. As each list shrinks, your self-esteem will grow.

Connecticut consultant Lucy Hedrick places all daily chores into one of four categories: phone calls, errands, things to write down, things to do. To keep track of them, she recommends two simple tools available in any dime store—a notebook and a pocket calendar.

Keep them handy, she advises. In the notebook, write headings for the four categories. Then enter your chores, big and small, as they come to mind.

"You shouldn't try to carry your life around in your head," Hedrick admonishes. "The reason you write things down is so you can free up your brain for more creative pursuits."

Keep Things Simple

Another way to get organized and to stay that way is to simplify your life.

A Barneys New York print ad gave some good advice on the subject: "Cross out half of everything you write. Don't say half of what you think. Get rid of half your clothes, furniture and friends. Answer questions true or false. Look on the bright side and if there isn't one, buy a flashlight."

Not enough time in the day to get it all done? The answer is obvious: *Make* time.

How?

TREAT TIME AS A PRECIOUS RESOURCE. Reapportion it. Quit spending it on the unimportant things in your life. So the laundry doesn't always get picked up. So the dinner wasn't as good as you could make it. Give yourself permission *not* to do everything perfectly, so you can do the important things well.

High personal standards are wonderful, but they don't have to apply to the nonessentials of your 24-hour-a-day existence. Accept the fact that your home won't always be spotless or your dinners always made completely from scratch. Regard dust as a protective coating for your furniture.

SEPARATE WHAT YOU CAN CONTROL FROM WHAT YOU CAN'T. Focus on what you *can* control. Forget the rest. "I'm much better at understanding what's my fault and what's someone else's," says freelance photographer Charlie Kloppenburg. "And I no longer worry about what's not my fault. You've no idea how much that has helped me."

QUIT DOING THINGS THE SAME OLD WAY. Question your habits. Do they still make sense in the context of your new life and your new priorities? It doesn't *have* to be the same old business at the same old stand. Take a close look at all the things you do habitually. Should you modify your expectations, your behavior? Are you doing a lot of things simply because you've always done them that way? What would happen if you got rid of a few of those old habits?

Fred Schultz, for example, is a traveling salesman who works out of his home. He habitually packed his suitcase for biweekly trips and meticulously unpacked when he got home. As a traveling salesman, it seemed the natural thing to do—get the clothes out of the suitcase and into the drawers, then repack them for the next trip. It never occurred to him that he didn't *have* to go through this meaningless routine over and over. One day, he was too tired to unpack when he got home, and he wound up leaving most of the contents of his suitcase right were they were. It made getting ready for his next trip, and coming home again, much more uncomplicated and pleasant.

So scrutinize your habits. They may have made perfect sense years ago, but do they still make sense now? Ask yourself: How many ways can I simplify my life? You may be surprised at the answers, and each one will buy you more time to spend on whatever's important to you right now.

HOUSEBREAKING THE PAPER LION

The analogy of a paper lion is an apt one, for paper can indeed devour you—and tear your sense of organization to shreds.

Remember when computers were coming into their own and experts predicted the paperless office? What arrived instead was the age of information. The reality today is we have more paper than ever to deal with. It seems to have taken on a life of its own, even propagating in the dark. (Why do some people love to fax while the rest of the world sleeps?)

We must become adept, therefore, at managing the flood of information that batters us in endless waves of bond, mimeo, and newsprint. It's vital to lowering stress, fostering productivity, and elevating efficiency in the home office.

The key to good paper management is an effective system for handling it, which is nothing more than implementing the right tools and instilling the proper work habits. The right tools vary, greatly or slightly, depending on one's profession, job, and industry. But proper habits apply to everyone.

Organization expert Sue Hurlbut's tips on taming the paper lion:

MAKE FILES, NOT PILES. Basically, there are two ways to file work for retrieval. One is a subject-activated system that classifies work by the type of activity. Headings such as "Top Priority," "To Read," "Bills to Pay," and "Projects" are some of the common ones. You record the type of activity on your calendar and then file the papers accordingly.

The other is a date-activated system driven by when you intend to do the work. Folders are labeled "1" through "31" and "Next Month."

The latter system organizes the work so it comes to your attention on the proper day and can be forgotten about until then. If you habitually work from a day planner or a "to do" list, the processes support and complement each other. Between the two, you know exactly what has to be done each day and what can wait.

If the date-activated system seems too rigid for you, come up with your own. The important thing is to get everything—except what you're working on right now—into one file or another, leaving both your mind and desk *clear* so you can concentrate on the task at hand.

This part is fairly easy. What's tougher is being able to retrieve whatever you need, quickly and effortlessly.

Understanding the nature of your work will help you determine which system best suits you. Some people deal with an endless procession of short-term tasks; dates and deadlines are critical to these individuals. Others handle fewer, longer-term projects; for them a system keyed to the type of activity works better. Still others have a natural affinity for efficiency and order, which may override any task-oriented considerations.

How do you decide which system is right for you? If you habitually work from a day planner or "to do" list, you'll probably prefer the subject-activated system. If you hate using a planner, chances are you'll be more at ease with a date-activated system.

USE IT OR LOSE IT. Skim through your incoming mail, magazines, and other materials, deciding which items require immediate or priority attention and which can be filed for later reference or action. Keep in mind that 80% of what most of us save never gets looked at again! Everything you store costs you money in rent, furniture, time, and space.

If you decide to hang onto the document, note clearly on it *what* has to be done and *when*, adding any information you think is pertinent. Then place the item in its proper file. Discard everything else.

There are only four choices: File it now; file it later; trash it now; trash it later. And now is always better than later.

SCHEDULE READING TIME. Set aside a block of time—not too large, say half an hour, each day or week, to read what you feel must be read. Then retain the perused material in a permanent file, or discard it. By systematically tending to this chore at a designated time you'll keep the pile manageable and not let it cut into your working day indiscriminately.

Good times to tackle the "To Read" file are just before or just after lunch, or before quitting for the day, when you're winding down. Don't blunt your momentum by doing it in the shank of the morning or afternoon.

Perhaps stick the file in your briefcase when you're headed for the doctor's office or on an out-of-town trip. Or take it to the bathtub if you're a soaker. Bring the file along whenever you anticipate some extra time on your hands.

SAVE ARTICLES, NOT ENTIRE PUBLICATIONS. Scan headlines and tables of contents of periodicals to identify articles of interest. Clip the items you want to read and store them in a file. Discard the rest of the publication. By saving only the articles, you can significantly reduce your paper volume.

CHAPTER SIX

An Office Is Not a Home: Necessary Boundaries

There's a hilarious scene in the 1983 movie *Never Cry Wolf.* The central character, a research scientist played by Charles Martin Smith, has been deposited alone in the Arctic wilderness to observe a pack of wolves at close range. Soon realizing he must stake out his own territory in the midst of their domain, he fills his bladder with tea and Moosehead beer, then marks a two-acre circle around his tent, tracing the borders of his turf in typical lupine fashion. The wolves promptly acknowledge his claim.

I'm not suggesting you get yourself a six-pack to circumscribe your office at home. Conventional demarcations will be just fine. What's important is that you clearly and distinctly, physically and emotionally, distinguish where you *work* from where you *live.*

The break is critical.

Home and Office: How *Not* to Blur the Boundaries

Be certain of one thing if both places exist under the same roof: An office is not a home, and vice versa. One space must not be allowed

65

to invade the other—not physically, if possible, and least of all in your mind.

Allow the boundaries to blur and you're in trouble—if not immediately, soon. You must have a *real* office, even if that reality exists only in your head.

It can be a place in or out of the house, even a specific table and chair at certain times of the day. Draw an imaginary line around that space and drum into your consciousness that when you're there, you're there to work. Nothing else!

Your Place of Business: Make It Professional

Amid all the hype, cautions *U. S. News & World Report* writer Leonard Wiener, "it's easy to assume that all you need to do to work at home successfully is set yourself up in a high-tech fully loaded office. In reality, you may do just fine with your grandfather's ancient roll-top desk, a high-quality typewriter, and the services of the local copy shop.

"But you risk losing your sanity and your credibility unless you take steps to turn your office into a professional place of business."

You must make it an office in every sense of the word: "A place," according to *Webster's*, "where a particular kind of business is transacted or a service supplied."

If the office has a door, keep it shut to everyone and everything irrelevant to your work.

Put up a sign if it reminds you of this fact. Brad Barton, an advertising copywriter, has "GENIUS AT WORK" tacked to his door. "I'm just trying to convince myself," he says with a grin. What's more important is that when he walks past that sign and through that door, he knows he's left *home* and gone to *work*.

MENTAL COMMUTING

Deliberately and consciously entering an area explicitly designated for work separates "being at home" from "being at the office," says Bruce Campbell, a New York graphic designer with a studio in his home. He calls it "mental commuting."

It's as important to cut yourself off from the blandishments of home as it is to wall off the allurements and distractions of the outside world.

Creating a Workplace That Suits Your Needs

You must create a "workplace" which is solely that.

It doesn't have to be a specific room or space. If you're one of those lucky people who can work well in many places, expand your universe accordingly. English playwright Alan Bennett says he can write in any room of his large London house, laboring just as happily in the dim, tiny-windowed basement as anywhere else.

INTENSELY PERSONAL PLACES. Most of us are more restricted in the way we work because we can't help ourselves.

Author Judith Krantz regards her writing room as such an intimate place, which she shares only with the characters who people her imagination, that she "gets furious when the window washers arrive."

Ann Landers feels the same way about her Chicago apartment high over Lake Michigan. Here, she paces from room to room, looking for inspiration and truth. "This is the only place where Ann Landers can deal with the problems of the country," reports *New York Times* correspondent Isabel Wilkerson. "She cannot do her work anywhere else."

There are no windows in the subterranean writing space Gay Talese calls his "bunker," a burrow deep under his Manhattan townhouse. The only view he wants is "that white piece of paper," he told *Harper's Bazaar*. That's his window to the world. "I don't want to see a stretch limousine or a great pair of ankles going by."

DIFFERENT SPACES FOR DIFFERENT WORK. Like British playwright Bennett, fundraiser Marcia Hoyt prefers to work in many places in her home. When she wants to "expand her mental horizons," she gravitates to an armchair with a majestic view of a river and the coastal range beyond.

On the other hand, the need for "focused, organizational thinking" moves her to a desk in the basement she describes as "nurturing and womb-like."

When the time comes for writing business proposals, reports, and time lines, Hoyt curls up in bed with her cat, a quadrille pad, and a cup of tea.

Author Fay Weldon also writes in bed. She does her first drafts "in an almost unconscious state," just after waking. Further drafts are also done in bed, Weldon reveals, but "in the clear daylight of the critical, as opposed to the creative, mind."

English novelist J. G. Ballard's working space is the living room of the small, drab house in a London suburb where he's lived these past 30-plus years and where he raised his children alone. "They had the rest of it, and I have this living room," says Ballard, whose autobiographical book, *Empire of the Sun*, was made into a 1987 movie by Steven Spielberg. The intriguing feature of the otherwise ordinary room is a large painting that leans against a wall. Ballard calls it his private garden, "where I go for a stroll."

Creating Mental Boundaries

Hoyt feels lucky she can move around the way she does. What kind of mental discipline, if any, permits her to be productive in such a fashion? "I don't ever let myself forget I'm *working*," she replies. "It's not where I am physically. It's where I am in my *head* that counts."

And so the boundaries must be set.

If you can't physically separate the space in which you work from the space in which you live, then you must cordon it off mentally and emotionally.

If your working space at home also serves as a living space at different times of the day or night—say, the kitchen table or a portion of the living room—then the task becomes that much harder. And even more vital to your success as a worker from home.

Note again that stilted phrase, "worker *from* home," rather than "worker *at* home." There's a world of difference between the two. One implies separateness, the other togetherness.

Where home offices are concerned, "together and apart" sums it all up.

Creating Physical Boundaries

Victor Martino, an economist and community planner, and Maggy Smith, a sculptor, have taken that maxim to the extreme. They are a two-career couple who live in one house and work in another. The two structures sit side by side on a slope overlooking Washington's Puget Sound. Why *two* buildings?

They find it "easier psychologically to concentrate on serious work in a studio and office that are apart from the main house," say Martino and Smith. Also, having a space that's strictly for business clearly separate home and business for the IRS, they told *Sunset* writer Nancy Davidson.

But how many home workers can afford such a luxury? Not too many, obviously. Pulitzer prizewinning journalist David Halberstam maintains his work space in a separate apartment at the rear of the building in which he lives on Manhattan's Upper West Side. He commutes to "the cage," as he calls it, to write on his word processor with Mozart or Jimmy Witherspoon playing in the background.

For the rest of his life, Jim Johnson, a former city commissioner and community college board member, plans to work from his 34-foot sailboat, doing construction work at various ports while he sails around the world continually, "floating from one adventure to the next," in his own words.

"It will be a life of self-sufficiency," says Johnson, 51, "rather than a life of spending half my time working to pay utilities and insurance companies."

The most important thing is that you *like* where you work because you're going to be spending a large chunk of your life there—alone. So, if you can't afford a separate house or apartment or a yacht as your office, can you convert part of your garage? Or a trailer or gazebo or barn or alcove or whatever else is available to you?

The point is, the word "office" implies a place "apart" for business, no matter what it looks like or what it actually is the rest of the time. If you're serious about working from home, one of the first things you'll do is stake out a real office. And the further you can position it mentally and emotionally from where you live, the better off you'll be.

The mental drill of disengaging business and work from home and hearth is essential to the person who hopes to incorporate them all into the same environment.

ON YOUR OWN: AWAY FROM HOME

An obvious option, if you can afford it, is to rent an office near your home, turning the 30-second commute into a longer one for personal reasons. Brian Kiernan did. He figured he had to from the outset. He knew himself too well to do otherwise.

The many years of getting up and going to the office were too ingrained, explains the former director of communications who jettisoned a six-figure salary to become, in his own words, "totally accountable to myself for my future successes and failures."

Going to the Office

Upon choosing to exit a 20-year corporate career, Kiernan chose to shell out several thousand dollars to equip a work space he maintains for another thousand a month in rent plus additional expenses at a pricey suburban business complex.

"It's how I work," he says simply.

Kiernan gives two other reasons for opting to work alone away from home. First, the financial investment imposes one more incentive for him to succeed. Second, he rationalizes that he achieves a more professional image than would come from having his teenage daughter answer the phone.

Like Kiernan, international marketing consultant John Bayer feels home and office should be separate and distinct, but far apart as well. Not for him the 30-second commute.

"The concept of 'going to work' is so ingrained in me that having a work space away from home is critical," says Bayer, who has been on his own for the past three years after a lifetime of working for others. "It's a mindset I can't shake."

Bayer seriously considered different working environments before settling into a "business incubator" in his area of town. He feels there's a "psychological switch" in his brain that still gets turned on when he's "headed for the office."

Printing broker Janet Livesay is another who can't combine home and office under the same roof. In fact, she actually feels guilty when she's home during working hours. Livesay, a printing broker who maintains a one-person office downtown, sometimes brings a few folders to the house to sort through in front of the TV, but never feels right about it.

"I have the uncomfortable feeling I'm not supposed to be here during the working day," she says. "I love my house," Livesay makes it clear. "I cherish it. I enjoy my garden. I don't even mind the housework. But I can't work here!"

The one exception is when she wakes up early and can't get back to sleep. It's only then that she can dip into her briefcase and work for an hour or two before setting off for her early morning workout at the downtown YMCA.

"I'm able to work at dawn but not in the evening," she muses, "because 3 or 4 in the morning is 'before' my working day, and 6 or 7 in the evening is 'after' my working day." She laughs. "Isn't that crazy? One's O.K. and the other isn't."

THE BENEFITS OF WORKING AWAY FROM HOME

Despite having an office in her comfortable suburban home, entertainment publicist Sandi Serling prefers to commute daily to a cubicle that her primary client provides for her at the company's corporate headquarters downtown.

"The action's downtown," explains Serling, 40, second cousin of famed actor/screenwriter Rod Serling and mother of an 8-year-old son and a 5-year-old daughter. "At home I feel out of the mainstream. I need to be with people, to work, chat, and have lunch with associates and friends. I need to hear things other than what my husband tells me," she says.

"I need the human contact, support, and reassurance on a daily basis. I need to stay on top of the nuances of my business, to be at the places I should be in my profession. You give up those things working from home."

Although Serling, Bayer, and Kiernan knew right off that a home office wasn't for them, it took freelance writer Susan

Middaugh 13 years of working under the family roof before she finally relented and rented space in a downtown professional building. In the August 1984 issue of *The Writer*, she gave these reasons for "Why You Need Your Own Office:"

1. *You get littering rights.* Whenever you quit working in a separate office, you can leave everything as it lies, ready and waiting to take up exactly where you left off. Dining room tables and other shared spaces in the home have to be cleared or neatened. Work materials have to be put away and dragged out repeatedly, adding to the lethargy of getting started each working day.

2. *It's all yours.* You have the key. You can come and go as you choose. With an office away from home, or one in the home that's strictly yours, you can set a working schedule based purely on your own physical and emotional biorhythms, free of anyone else's concerns and considerations.

3. *You're taken more seriously.* Right, wrong, or irrelevant, by going to an office you automatically earn more respect from friends, relatives, and most importantly, yourself.

4. *It's an added incentive.* With the additional overhead of a rented office, you're less likely to ease up or goof off. Rented space provides a daily reality check: "You're in business and don't forget it!" Consider the investment an act of faith in your commitment to succeed.

5. *It's tax-deductible.* As far as the IRS is concerned, a rented office elevates you from the rank of amateur to a full-fledged professional. If you work from home, unless the space is a separate structure used solely for business, the amount and even the eligibility of your tax write-off could be questioned. Office rent, on the other hand, is fully and undeniably tax-deductible.

6. *It's more businesslike.* No matter how solid you think your business relationships may be or whether your services are highly creative in nature, it's generally better to do business in an office than a living room. Regardless of how *you* feel about it, clients are usually more comfortable conferring in a traditional setting.

Rational or not, the feeling could be that your products or services are worth less because you don't generate them in a real office. If you don't have a formal place in which to meet, insist on visiting clients at their locations. Or suggest a convenient restaurant.

7. *It's a better environment.* From both a mental and emotional standpoint, an office away from home is more conducive to productivity simply because it's a place designated for "work." Consciously and unconsciously, you'll respond to the surrounding sights, sounds, and very vibrations. They should bolster your professional attitude and work ethic. Also, if you're in a downtown office, you'll be that much closer to business resources and associates. And taking a break will be just that—a real change of scenery and activity.

Too Close to Comfort

Maggie Medford had to alter her dream of working alone. She found it every bit as rewarding as she'd anticipated. But not at home. It took her a month to decide on renting a midtown office. "I was too close to the kitchen, the sofa, the TV, the novel I was reading," Medford explains. "I realized early on it wasn't going to work, that I had to separate my work from the comforts of home. I knew I had to leave home and go to work because I didn't have the self-discipline to keep the two together but apart."

Separate and distinct they must be, if not across town, then down the hall or up the stairs, at least in the corridors of your mind.

Home is a place of nurturance, refuge, and recuperation, while the essence of the traditional workplace is performance and productivity, points out Roxane Farmanfarmaian in *Psychology Today*. "When the two zones overlap, steps must be taken to see that each is preserved or enhanced, not diminished, by the presence of the other."

Some Must Modify the Dream

Like it or not, working from home may not be your most prudent option despite comprising the heart of your dream. The bosom of one's family is, indeed, a wonderful, nurturing place to be, but not necessarily when you're trying to get some work done. Nonetheless, if you're bound and determined to succeed in an office in your home, this book will help you achieve that commendable end.

For those, however, who have bowed to expediency as the better part of valor, a few words of commiseration. I too envisioned working happily from an office in my home, but the dream evaporated the same day school let out during that first summer of being on my own. Suddenly I was awash in preteen and teenage children—mine—and facing a crushing deadline with nowhere to hide. The very next day I rented a workspace for the magnificent sum of $75 a month, to which I commuted for the next six years. Only many years later have I come to realize how perfectly it suited my needs.

Jonathan Nicholas, a local newspaper columnist did a piece on me titled "Paregoric Parachute," describing my solitary working environment back in those lean and hungry years. "Now he spends his working days in a tiny room in an apartment building on N.W. Johnson Street," wrote Nicholas. "The view from the solitary window is so bad he keeps his curtain closed all day. There is no Xerox machine in the corner. No coffee machine in the corridor. No IBM Selectric wanting to be ever-so-lightly stroked, purring as contentedly as a twice-fed cat. Instead he perches on an old kitchen chair, hunched over the keys of a 1911 Underwood manual that he picked up at a garage sale for $25."

For Some Work Ethics, Spartan Is Better than Luxurious

One day, soon after the column ran, my oldest son Mike, who's married now and a working journalist himself, stopped by to visit me in my office. I remember putting my arm on his shoulder as he gazed around that dim, drab room and whispering in his ear, "Some day, son, this will all be yours." He still laughs out loud at the memory.

In retrospect, however, everything about that awful, unreposing office was exactly right for me. It was a place to which I went to work and a place from which I left to go home again, just as I'd done five days a week for 20 ingrained years. It was a place where

I could spread everything out and come back the next day to find it all the way I left it. There was no couch, no TV set, no well-stocked fridge or pantry to lure me away from the business at hand. Best of all, it was all mine, a place where I went to shut out the world and do some of the best work of my life.

I've worked from home ever since and I've learned to be as happy and productive here as I was in that tiny, spartan office by the laundry room on the ground floor of a decrepit apartment building. But I sometimes wonder how long I'd have lasted on my own if I hadn't wound up in that miserable, glorious place on N.W. Johnson.

THE FOUR WALLS OF YOUR MIND

For the homeworker, physically structuring a definite work zone within the residence must be a vital priority. But, by far, the biggest challenge is psychological. It involves rearranging one's emotions as well.

It means enclosing yourself in the four walls of your mind, whether or not the actual walls of your office exist.

It means keeping where you live separate and distinct from where you work because they're under the same roof.

Something that may help is to remind yourself constantly: I work *from* home, not *at* home.

There's a keen difference.

Your decision to work from the home, whether full- or part-time, will have other complex ramifications, Roxanne Farmanfarmaian cautions: "It will alter the pace and texture of your days, bringing into the domestic zone of home, hearth, and family the strictures and imperatives of the work zone."

The responsibility for keeping them separate rests strictly with you.

STRUCTURING A WORK ZONE

For people such as Medford, Kiernan, and others on their own, whether in solitary offices inside or outside the home, New Jersey

Institute of Technology's Miriam K. Mills stresses the use of "microflow" activities to provide structure and purpose to otherwise random experiences.

Such activities, she explains, are "arbitrary patterns used to give shape to a task and provide a respite from boredom and anxiety." Examples from the corporate world: deeply carpeted rooms for ceremonial meetings, elegant furniture, heavy stock paper, imposing name plates.

These are symbols, says Mills, that serve as road markers and points of demarcation for career progress and suitable forms of interaction.

"The individual working at home," she notes, "still requires the same texture of microflow activity that he or she would experience at the job site."

Dress for Success

It's important, for instance, to *dress* suitably for work, even if that work takes place in your own living room—make that *because* it's your own living room.

What about the guy, you ask, who starts working in his pajamas every morning to assure himself a fast start? Well, that's him, and you're you. And if working in your pajamas or a bathrobe or leotards or in the buff succeeds for you, then do it.

At the risk of belaboring a point, I'll say it again: Try what has worked for others. But decide, as only you can, what works for *you*.

If you're the inevitable exception to the rule, good for you. But finding your own answers should start with checking out other people's successess—the tried and true, the reliable and proven.

Good grooming and proper attire are part of Mills' microflow activities. They play a real part in business success for most people because they strongly affect one's self-image. They're all the more important to solitary workers, who have no one else around to influence what they think of themselves.

Pierre Cardins or YMCA Sweats? Author Talese usually wears a three-piece Italian suit in the isolation of his insulated bunker. In his own mind, he told a magazine writer, his sartorial elegance reflects itself in the impeccability of his prose. As does the gold fountain pen he uses to scrawl his final drafts.

"There's no way I'm going to put on a Pierre Cardin suit to work in my basement office," you protest.

Why not? "Because I don't need to! I'm a pharmaceutical rep, for cryin' out loud!"

Fair enough. Why not wear the sweats you ran in last night, then? "I wouldn't feel *right*. After all, I talk to clients all day on the phone."

But they can't see you. "I still wouldn't feel right."

What do you usually wear? "Slacks, loafers, a sports shirt."

Are they clean? "Certainly!"

Do you shower, brush your teeth, and comb your hair before going to work? "Of course I do! Otherwise I'd feel like a slob."

There you go.

What's that old saying? "Handsome is as handsome does." Liken it to smiling when you talk on the phone. Grinning into the receiver really does make you sound more pleasant.

It's like the feeling you get just after you've washed and waxed your car. The old heap just seems to run better. You can't explain why, but it does, doesn't it? At least it seems to, which is what really counts, right?

Absolutely!

Maintain Regular Hours

Another good rule for people on their own is to adhere to regular working hours. Adhere to a performance schedule as rigidly as you do a dress code.

Try to put the same number of hours into your own business as you'd contribute if you worked for someone else. But have the hours suit you; that's a privilege of being your own boss. And keep your schedule constant.

"I'm in the office at 9 A.M. sharp," says research consultant Laurie Brown-Nagin. "No matter what else is going on in the house, I ignore it. I just go into my office."

Some solitary workers keep a log of their working hours to help them manage themselves more efficiently. And to alert them to make necessary adjustments in the time spent at "home" vs. the office.

Don't cut out early just because you've gotten the day's work done. At least not too often because it could get to be a habit. And you might find yourself doing it regardless of the workload still staring you in the face.

Stay Flexible

Keep in mind, however, that your hours needn't be inflexible, just regular. Feel free to adapt your working habits to your changing lifestyle and evolving self-awareness. Not only is it your privilege, it's a good idea to tailor your working hours to your own biorhythms and even your biological clock.

Nothing is forever. Only change is constant.

So go with the flow—your own.

Remember, you can do anything *you* want to do—work Friday through Tuesday, if you like, and take Wednesdays and Thursdays off. Or work in the morning, seven days a week. Or just on weekends.

What's important is that your regimen fits you, and of course, suits the kind of work you do. Just be faithful to your prevailing schedule.

Don't Mix Work and Leisure

It's also a good idea to go somewhere else to eat and do non-work-related activities you must attend to during your working day.

Fran FitzSimon, whose graphic design studio takes up the second-floor landing and an adjoining computer-crammed bedroom, never snacks upstairs.

And if there's a dinner party to get ready for that day, she'll do it on her lunch hour—downstairs. And she does mean *hour*—*one* hour—and then it's back to work. Upstairs. Until 6:00, when her husband comes home.

Her office is not her home, FitzSimon makes it clear. Or vice versa.

They may occupy the same physical terrain, but they're emotional and psychological poles apart. For her, the twain don't meet. And never mix if she can help it.

STRATEGIC WITHDRAWALS

What's smart, too, is to get away from your place of business once in a while. Leave the office so it doesn't get to feel all-confining, so you'll be eager to jump in again when you get back.

Stroll downstairs, into the backyard, or around the block. Go up the street. Stop for a latte. Sit in the park.

Assign yourself small trips, suggests *Writer's Digest* columnist Art Spikol: "People who work at home will understand. You go to the bank, the post office, a nearby luncheonette for a lonely lunch.

"You promise yourself that after you finish three more pages, you can do something really interesting, like jog or take the dog for a walk, and if you don't have a reason for going out, you invent one."

Knowing When to Quit

It's as important to know when to quit for the day, when to lock up and go home. Back downstairs.

There's another risk for people on their own—the flip side of habitually quitting work too early. It's the danger that unfinished business will chew up larger and larger chunks of your time, start to swallow up parts of your evenings and weekends.

As a self-employed worker, you know full well that if the projects don't get done, you won't get paid. Fifty-hour, 60-hour, and even 70-hour weeks may become standard operating procedure.

Then people start calling you the "W" word. It has nasty implications. Because being a workaholic leaves precious little time for anything else such as nurturing relationships, recharging your physical and emotional batteries, enjoying life and all that other good stuff you work to support.

Don't let it happen to you, even if your clients would love you for becoming a workaholic.

Leave Promptly

When it's time to leave the office, do it promptly.

Don't hang around to read a novel or make personal phone calls. Use the couch and the extension in the living room. Some people have a separate business phone with its own recorder, and they only pick it up during business hours. If you're afraid you'll miss a client's call, check the answering machine later.

Do work-related activities in the office during working hours. Do home-related things at home when you get there. If you're going to work late, stay in the office. If you're going to quit early, leave. Go home.

"Home" may be up or down a flight of stairs, but it should be a considerable distance in your mind. When you leave the office, close the door behind you. More importantly, shut the door in your head. Leave the work where it belongs, in the office. Don't drag it into the house with you.

A specific time and place for work isn't about regimentation. It's about creating a model of behavior that fosters optimum productivity. It's about adhering to a regular routine so the adrenaline starts flowing—and shuts down—on schedule.

It's about a place for everything—and everything in its place.

CHAPTER SEVEN

EXTINGUISHING PROCRASTINATION: LIGHTING A FIRE UNDER YOURSELF

You know you're in trouble when you notice the dishes in the sink and suddenly it's the most important thing in the world that you wash them. And put them away. Next thing you know, you've got the vacuum cleaner out. Then you're emptying the clothes dryer. Suddenly it's noon. Damn, where did the morning go?

But not to worry. You're a professional. An old hand at working alone—motivated, organized, disciplined, tested, proven. Besides, look at everything you got done, you tell yourself, ignoring the small voice in your head that reminds you, "You mean, besides your *work*?"

So you do what most experienced home workers resort to under fire, when a relentless deadline stares them in the eye. You have lunch.

Finally you're ready.

For a nap.

And so it goes.

SNAP THE ELASTIC DEADLINE

Being too close to the washer and dryer is a problem for freelance writer Susan Hauser, whose home office comprises a computer desk, word processor, phone, fax machine, and overflowing bookcase that flanks the length of one wall in her unheated garage. "I'm about six feet away from the washer and dryer, which makes it real handy," she notes with a grin. "Problem is, they're *too* handy."

Hauser realizes she's in trouble when she starts tending to housework instead of business. "I'll have a cluttered mind if I have a cluttered house," she tells herself. Or "I can't work with the kitchen so messy." And she winds up cleaning.

But she knows she's just making excuses for not getting down to business.

"Messy house, messy mind," is what Barbara Borden tells herself as she dusts and cleans when she ought to be pushing computer keys instead of a Hoover. Like Hauser, the 37-year-old economist's reasoning is that she has to tidy her working environment before she can straighten her thoughts. But neatness isn't her problem. It's procrastination.

The insidious Elastic Deadline.

Don't Live for Tomorrow

Different people have different names for it, all derisive. In the military it's called dereliction of duty, a court martial offense. Business managers fire employees who do it too often. It's treated like a social disease, scorned as a character flaw. Those afflicted by it are considered weak, shiftless, unreliable. As children, they're known as dawdlers. As adults, they're called ditherers.

We're talking about procrastinators. The tomorrow people, for whom *mañana* never comes. They put things off. Constantly. They stop and smell the roses. Too often, and too long. They're the people still shopping on Christmas Eve, those poor souls lined up at the post office on April 15th with their tax returns.

In an impatient world that seldom encourages them, "Go ahead, take your time," what they usually hear is, "Get off your butt, you haven't got all day!" They have utterly no sense of responsibility bewail their spouses, no idea of the consequence of their let-the-world-go-by attitude. Their motto: "If it isn't fun, do it later." Better yet, don't do it at all.

Trouble is, they don't enjoy their procrastination. That nagging inner voice won't let them. They're ashamed, miserable, guilt-ridden. They drive themselves crazy along with everyone else.

SOMETIMES IT'S SMART TO PROCRASTINATE— WHAT TO DO WHEN IT'S NOT

It's important to realize that we all procrastinate at times. In fact, there are occasions, suggests behavior analyst Katherine Klotzburger, when it's *smart* to procrastinate.

Really?

Delay making a difficult phone call, for instance, when you're angry or upset and you'll handle the problem better once you've cooled off. Put off buying something and you'll probably pay less later. When you're dragging your heels for no apparent reason, your sixth sense might just be sounding a silent alarm to tread slowly.

Then again, you just may be dogging it.

How do you know when it's O. K. to procrastinate and when it's not?

"Ask what will happen if you never do what you're postponing," advises Klotzburger. "Is the outcome likely to be better or worse than getting it done?"

Of course, you can postpone even asking yourself these questions, then you'll know for sure you're a procrastinator.

And what if you really are one?

Handle the Problem!

What if you know you ought to be doing something and you still put it off again and again?

Well, then, you're in trouble—serious trouble if you work alone. And you'd better fix the problem. Or go to work for someone else, preferably a real dictator, because you probably won't make it on your own.

Procrastination is the foremost reason people never reach their personal and professional goals. They put off trying until it's too late, letting their golden chances drift by. Following through on one's good intentions may not always result in a successful out-come, but it assures a life of fewer regrets.

Failure won't kill you. But not trying might.

We procrastinate, say the experts, because the task *bores* or *scares* us. Another reason, claims time-management consultant Lucy Hedrick, is we don't *reward* ourselves enough for performing the necessary, thankless chores in our lives.

"If a job well done was always rewarded," says Hedrick, author of *Five Days to An Organized Life*, "we'd all be so high from working there would be no such thing as procrastination."

Reward Yourself for a Job Well Done

Marcia Hoyt agrees. "Joy or at least a measure of enjoyment should be the main motivating force in our lives each day," says the 47-year-old marketing consultant who has worked alone most of her life.

To combat procrastination, she makes a concerted effort to schedule periodic "rewards" into her daily and weekly routines: Lunches, dinners, "something pleasant" with friends; regular workouts at her health club; evening phone calls to her mother; a mid-morning and mid-afternoon dose of CNN "to keep in touch with the world at large;" a climactic hour or two in her beloved garden on summer afternoons.

Keep firmly in mind, though, that a reward is given as the *result* of a commendable action—not *instead* of it. *Webster's New Collegiate Dictionary* defines "reward" as "something that is offered or given for some service or attainment." A second definition affirms the wisdom of rewarding oneself when it is deserved: "A stimulus administered to an organism following a correct or desired response that increases the probability of occurrence of the response."

Don't Accept Substitutes

There are procrastinators who attempt to justify their gold-bricking by substituting activities that would be commendable if they weren't replacing a more suitable action. The word "insidious" (as in Insidious Elastic Deadline) fits this type of procrastination perfectly. Going back to the dictionary, we find this adjective defined as "harmful but enticing; awaiting a chance to entrap."

Entrapment is exactly what happens to malingerers who indulge in activities which, in their own mind, justify shirking work. Commendable goldbricking solves nothing, of course. It just makes a bad thing, well, not quite so bad.

Tending to housework instead of business is a common ploy for malingerers who earn their living where they live. When they're through dusting and cleaning and washing, the other work's still there, waiting, with even less time to get it done. But at least the house is clean, they tell themselves.

Musician/accountant Ron Kogen indulges in this form of procrastination by fixing himself an elaborate meal or baking a pie when he should be working. "I'm aware it isn't the time to be cooking and I shouldn't be doing it," he says. "Yet I rationalize that I'm getting something *constructive* done, and so it isn't procrastination. Not really. But of course it is," Kogen acknowledges with a sheepish grin.

Shun Creative Malingering

For insurance adjuster Fred Sachs, a prebreakfast jog to energize himself for his workday at home evolved into a major drain on his productivity. Because he found this healthful but time-consuming and physically tiring activity pleasurable and emotionally rewarding, he began extending his runs. They soon evolved from a prelude to the shank of his day.

In reality, his 7- to 12-mile runs not only gave him a false sense of achievement but also blunted his daily momentum, diverting vital energy from the less-enjoyable but more-important work awaiting him. Sachs finally got his priorities straight by becoming a late-afternoon runner, putting the cart where it belonged—behind the horse, the labor before the reward.

Like Sachs, Jim Rooney rationalized a pleasurable activity into a major tap on his valuable time. A soothing, mind-clearing soak in the tub was just the ticket for launching into a productive day, figured the 58-year-old community planner.

Sounds reasonable enough, and it was, until Rooney postponed pulling the plug as he soaked, read, soaked, dozed, and soaked some more while the morning seeped away. He finally imposed a bathing curfew on himself—30 minutes max! Now, aside from an occasional relapse, he's dressed and ready for work at a reasonable time.

What to Do When the Cures Become the Problems

Like Sachs's and Rooney's good intentions gone astray, what started as a restorative interlude for marketing consultant Marge Kramer mushroomed into a major drag on her productivity. She began taking catnaps—short pauses that refreshed and revived her. Fair enough.

But the naps grew more frequent and longer in duration. Sleep became an irresistible drug to her, so much so that for a while she thought she'd contracted narcolepsy.

It took a major effort, she relates, to resist her daytime drowsiness, once she'd repeatedly succumbed to it. She started by declaring her bed off-limits, reasoning that a flop on the couch wouldn't be as comfortable and serve to shorten the siestas. Then she allowed herself to stretch out only on the rug, figuring that would cut down on her napping even more. And it did.

Finally she quit snoozing altogether, forcing herself to remain at her desk through the siren calls of Morpheus—making phone calls, when necessary, to stave off her drowsiness.

"I'm a recovering napper," she admits with a laugh. "I know that just a quick one will knock me off the wagon."

WHAT TYPE OF PROCRASTINATOR ARE YOU?

How do we procrastinate? Katherine Klotzburger counts the ways by pigeonholing the tomorrow people:

1. *Perfectionists*, who set their sights so high they intimidate themselves into failing. They postpone tackling the Herculean

tasks they've set for themselves until it's too late. Their common gripe: "I could have made it if I'd had enough time."

2. *Adventurers*, who create continual crises in their lives because they're hooked on hairpin chases and hairbreadth finishes. It's their way of slaking the thirst for a sense of self-importance that adrenaline-charged situations inject into their lives. These people should take up skydiving or bungee-jumping so they can settle down and work sensibly.

3. *Rebels*, who vent their anger by promising things they can't deliver, and then make sure they don't by procrastinating. It's their way of expressing dissatisfaction—to themselves and others in authority—without risking an open confrontation or addressing the real problem with a viable solution.

4. *Decidophobics*, who can't bear to make decisions because they're afraid of what could result. So they stall, hoping the risk and responsibility will be taken out of their hands.

Procrastination's Tell-Tale Tip-Offs

Aside from understanding *why* you procrastinate, if that's what you're prone to do, learn to recognize *when* you procrastinate, so you can nip it in the bud. A good warning sign is guilt, points out professional organizer Sue Hurlbut. Guilt, she says, tells you:

1. You're not doing what you *ought* to be doing.
2. You're letting yourself down by not living up to your standards, by not doing as well as you can, for yourself or for a client.
3. You're disappointing someone.
4. Worst of all, you're getting yourself into trouble—with a customer, your lawyer, your accountant, the IRS...

It's your psyche giving you a sharp nudge, letting you know you're messing up by goofing off!

How to Combat Procrastination

Procrastination, Ron Kogen readily admits, is his biggest problem, usually taking the form of "just enjoying" himself when he ought to be working. But he doesn't really enjoy himself when he ought to be working, he confesses, because it's important for him to feel productive, to generate activities that afford him satisfaction and a sense of accomplishment. He feels depressed otherwise. And he realizes fully that disliking himself for tasks not done in a timely manner siphons his vitality and joy.

Respect Your Work Ethic

It's important, therefore, to acknowledge your work ethic. Accept that unless you earn your leisure, you're not going to enjoy it. It's simply the way we are. All of us. We need to be busy and productive to be happy, to feel fulfilled.

Even for today's youth, a generation whose outlook on career paths has changed radically from their parents' and grandparents' regard for work, the ultimate insult is to be called a "slacker."

Go back to the dictionary. You'll find "slacker" defined as "a person who shirks work or duty." It's a slur that people in their 20s take offense at as strongly as people in their 30s, 40s and 50s. Today's twentysomethings will accept the label if it describes members of their generation taking their time to find what they *really* want to do with their lives. But don't accuse them of terminal malingering. It's a bum rap, they say.

As Texas filmmaker Richard Linklater once put it to a reporter, "It's not avoiding responsibility; it's finding your own path through this maze of programming and pressures." The way so many other people on their own are doing today.

Fight Your Own Battle

Ron Kogen knows what he has to do about his procrastination. "I have to accomplish more early in the day, not pick up *The New York Times* first thing and read it from cover to cover," he says.

"Instead of doing the easy, routine tasks first because they're simple, I need to attack the hard stuff right off, the things I've been avoiding. I need to get *into* them, get 'em done and out of the way. Time flies by once I'm involved. It's just a matter of getting started."

There's an old English proverb Kogen says he's taken to heart: "The shortest answer is *doing*."

TEN WAYS TO KICK PROCRASTINATION

1. *Harness guilt.* Put your self-recrimination to work! Make yourself pay royally when you procrastinate. Don't deny your bad feelings or mitigate them. Remind yourself that the saddest words of pen or tongue are Kahlil Gibran's "It might have been." Worse than not achieving an important goal is having only yourself to blame for failing.

Then work through your guilt by vowing to make better use of your time in the future. Tell yourself, as French journalist Jean-Louis Servan-Schreiber reminds us, that time, like any other resource, is readily available. But unlike other resources, time can't be bought or sold, borrowed or stolen, stocked or saved, manufactured, reproduced, or modified.

"All we can do," Servan-Schreiber points out, "is make use of it."

Or not.

And the ultimate loss when we don't make use of time—when it finally runs out—lies in not having spent our share of it well. That's the psychological burden procrastinators have to carry. If you're one of them, let the remorse lie heavy on your shoulders. You may eventually decide it's not worth the ache and pain.

"Get into the here and now," urges physician David D. Burns, author of *The Feeling Good Handbook*. "Don't worry about everything you have to do in the future. Life exists one minute at a time, so all you have to do at any given time is one minute's worth of work."

2. *Be realistic.* Accept, as M. Scott Peck advises, that life *is* hard and will pose endless challenges. They will never stop coming, so face up to the fact that you'll have to gear up to meet them again and again.

Don't assume that successful people blithely succeed without their share of frustration, trial and error, self-doubt, and above all, *effort*. Tell yourself that, like them, you will have to achieve your goals the old-fashioned way—through daily hard work and perseverance.

"Highly productive people *know* that life is frustrating," observes physician/author David Burns. "They *assume* they'll encounter obstacles; when they do, they persevere until they overcome them."

3. *Do it now*. Remind yourself the ideal time to do anything is usually right away. If something must be done, it's best to get started immediately. What's more, cautions George H. Lorimer, "Putting off an easy thing makes it hard, but putting off a hard one makes it impossible." So don't wait for the spirit to move you. Inspiration is the worst procrastinator of them all. It's never there when you need it most.

4. *Know when and why you're procrastinating*. Learn to recognize the warning signs so you can make detours well ahead of the potential roadblocks. Are you starting to putter or fuss with housework? Are you really hungry or just looking for an excuse to stop working? Are you trying to convince yourself there's more than enough time to complete the project on deadline when there really isn't?

The rest is relatively easy. Once you've identified when and why you tend to malinger, you can go around your danger areas. But start right away. The insidious thing about procrastination is it can become a habit, one that feeds greedily on itself.

"Simply put," says New York psychotherapist Theodore Kurtz, "the more you procrastinate, the more you procrastinate. Chronic procrastinators frequently put off doing even things they enjoy. Once it becomes an ingrained habit, procrastination becomes increasingly less selective."

5. *Eliminate the negatives*. Next time you start avoiding a task that has to be done, check to see whether you're feeding yourself negative thoughts: "Why should I even bother, there isn't

enough time." "I'm not really qualified to handle this." "The client's not paying me enough for the project."

If so, substitute "can do" feelings: "There may not be enough time, but I really have to try!" "I can do this as well as anyone if I give it my best shot!" "I'm not getting paid as much as I should for this, but if I do a good job I can get the client to make up for it on the next project."

Remind yourself of the benefits that will result from getting off your duff and forging ahead—how good you'll feel afterwards. Your change of attitude should make a world of difference. If it doesn't, take a hard look at what you're trying so hard to get yourself to do. Is it worth the effort?

"There's nothing so useless," observes Peter F. Drucker, "as doing efficiently that which should not be done at all."

If the task has to be done, ask yourself if it should be done by *you*. Can you delegate or postpone it? Will the benefits of completing the chore outweigh the benefits of putting it off? If not, maybe you *should* delay. Do you really need more time, more facts, more deliberation before proceeding? What are the chances the problem will solve itself if you leave it alone a while longer?

Answer these questions honestly, and then act accordingly. But *act*, one way or the other.

6. *Clear the decks.* If there's something you feel you really ought to be doing instead of working, such as writing a long overdue letter or making a personal phone call, go ahead and take care of it! Or promise yourself you will later. But get whatever it is that's preoccupying you off your mind, off your chest, off your conscience, or off wherever else it has you pinned down, so you can move ahead.

If you find yourself thinking in a vicious circle, or you're feeling depressed or anxious or panicky, face up to whatever's bothering you and resolve to fix it. Only by acknowledging the problem will you extricate yourself from it.

Anxiety and depression, whatever their causes, not only mire us in feelings of helplessness and despair but also serve to stifle our memory and make us extremely susceptible to distractions. A recent study, however, reveals that depressed individuals, using simple techniques to refocus their attention, do just as well on memory tests as nondepressed people.

So come to a decisive stand on what's bothering you, whether or not it results in immediate remedial action. Belly up to the problem by resolving to handle it. The conscious decision will free you to concentrate on the obligations at hand.

Aside from satisfying your mental and emotional demands, take care of your physical needs as well, advises pharmaceutical sales rep Julie Stream. "When I settle down to work, I don't want to be hungry or thirsty or too warm or too cold or needing to go to the bathroom. I have to be comfortable. My mind has to say, 'Look, you're ready now! You've got no more excuses, so quit fighting and just do it!'"

7. *Get yourself moving.* Do whatever it takes to overcome the blahs, to get energized, to get started, and to keep moving. Only you know where all your buttons are stashed and what pushes them. Go back and read about fast starts; they're the best way to sidestep and outdistance procrastination.

Enlist whatever aids you need to mow down this dark usurper of your time and productivity. If it's guilt, grab hold and hang on tight. "If, like me, you're one of the unlucky ones driven by guilt," says Janet Burroway, "then welcome your guilt and make sure it drives you toward the desk rather than away."

What works for Ron Kogen is being a clock-watcher. When he finds himself checking the time repeatedly, he knows it's because he ought to be working. "Each time I glance at the clock, it reminds me I haven't done anything but have breakfast and read the paper. If I do it often enough, it usually gets me going."

So he has six clocks in his two-bedroom condo where he maintains an office in a corner of the dining room. This way, every time he looks up, he sees the time. Excessive? He'd get a dozen clocks, he says, if they'd be twice as effective for him.

8. *Pick the right time.* "Perform each task at the most suitable time, when you can accomplish it most effectively," advises Michigan time/space/information management specialist Dorothy Lehmkuhl, who serves on the board of the National Association of Professional Organizers.

"Schedule activities you consider mentally or physically challenging for your peak-energy times," she counsels. "This includes making tough decisions. Do the jobs you enjoy, even if you consider them hard work, at low-ebb times.

"And don't set yourself up to fail by trying to accomplish difficult work against impossible odds," she concludes. "When you know, for example, that you'll have too many interruptions to do a good job on the project you've set for yourself, don't schedule it. Again, choose the best time for each task."

9. *Put stress to good use.* Too much stress is bad for you, acknowledges psychologist Al Siebert, co-author of *The Adult Student's Guide to Survival and Success.* "But a certain amount of it is necessary for health, well-being, and learning," he advises. "Professional training programs build competence by pushing people to their limits. And stressful experiences can motivate individuals to develop new coping skills."

Learn to deal with the internal pressures and emotional strain you'll encounter working alone, Dr. Siebert suggests, by clearly identifying everything you regard as negative, frustrating, and upsetting in your life. Make a list of them. By simply writing them down, you will have taken the first step toward dealing with these pressures. You'll have put yourself in greater control.

Now go through the list, item by item, and ask yourself: How much control do I have over this event or circumstance? Can I do something about it? Can I improve the situation in any way? Exactly what *can* I do, if anything? Is there someone who can help me? What if I change my attitude? Why is this thing bad? Or is it really good for me?

Next, says Siebert, make a second list identifying what you consider to be positive and rewarding. Put down which activities make you happy and relaxed, what makes you feel good, what you enjoy doing, the things you're enthusiastic about.

Then ask yourself: Am I ignoring or taking for granted some positive aspects of my life and work? What personal and professional things would I like to do that I keep putting off? Is there a good reason not to indulge myself in them?

The objective, Siebert concludes, is to clearly identify both the negative and positive aspects of your life. Doing so will help you accentuate those positives and eliminate the negatives, as the old song goes. Together they should point the way to what you have to do, and what you have to *quit* doing. It's a short step from there to taking some action.

10. *Reward yourself when you deserve it.* If you don't, who will? Make it worth your while not to procrastinate—the greater the effort, the sweeter the compensation. Pay yourself for a job well done, whether it's a hearty pat on the back or a more substantial treat.

"Schedule intermissions in your work," suggests graduate student Andy Fisher. "With regular interludes to look forward to, you'll stick to the program you've set for yourself. You'll be less likely to take those innumerable impulsive breaks that are so disruptive to your concentration," he advises.

"But when you're working, be intolerant about interruptions," exhorts Fisher. "Once the computer's booted up, ignore the phone, the TV, the snacks—unless they're scheduled. Work is business. And business always comes before recreation."

There are exceptions that validate this solid rule, however. Financial analyst/soccer aficionado Paul Steward is a case in point. During the 1994 World Cup, staged in the United States for the first time ever, Stewart set a special schedule for himself. He vowed to watch all 52 of the televised World Cup games—and almost succeeded in his pleasurable goal. He fell short by only three matches. "I'm a soccer nut," explains Steward, a full-time telecommuter who works from his home. "I grew up playing the game in the Philippines. I just *had* to see every match, regardless of the consequences. Incredibly, though, I got a tremendous amount of work done despite taking as many as three two-hour breaks a day to watch all the scheduled matches. Of course, I stayed up pretty late some nights catching up on my work."

Niles made a pact with himself, one that he faithfully honored. During the month-long course of the tournament, he would work seven-day weeks but sandwich the work around the games. He gave himself permission to watch every single game regardless of what time of the day or night it was televised, as long as he dutifully completed his daily quota of business before and after each match.

"It was wonderful," Niles reports, eyes still gleaming at the memory. "I wish I could have done it all year. The games were both a glorious incentive and a magnificent reward for getting my work done as quickly and efficiently as possible. I was a tireless worker. I didn't give procrastination a first, much less a second thought."

Turning CAN'Ts Into CANs

When you find yourself procrastinating, advises Sue Hurlbut, sort through all the reasons you *can't* do what you're supposed to be doing and find the one or two things you *can* do. Then get started on them. Dislodging a single obstacle can free a logjam. For example:

If You Can't	*Can You*
Develop the brochure because you feel you don't have enough time . . .	Go ahead and look at other brochures, note what you like and jot down a few ideas?
Undertake the project, run the business or whatever it is you can't handle . . .	Read a book, take a class, confer with an expert or hire a consultant?
Afford the money to get the work done . . .	Talk to someone about trading skills?

"Every *can't* has a matching *can*," says Hurlbut. "We just have to find it."

Clear the Way for Action

Getting clear in your mind exactly what it is you have to do usually allows you to move forward. Most large projects, claims Hurlbut, can be broken down into tasks that fall into specific categories:

- If the task involves people, there are phone calls to be made and individuals to see. Make a list and start dialing.
- If it involves things to secure, there are items to assemble. Make a list and start moving.

- If it involves things to do, decide what you'll handle and what you'll delegate. Make a list for each category.
- If it involves deadlines, draw up a timetable for each segment of the project. Make sure every task can be completed in the allotted time.
- If the project involves money, prepare budgets, cost estimates, billable time, and so on. Make sure they're reasonable projections. Get necessary approvals.

Assign Each Task a Deadline

Tips on breaking down projects:

- Enter your headings on a piece of paper, randomly listing whatever has to be done. Put down all tasks as soon as they come to mind so you don't miss any. Worry about prioritizing them later.
- Estimate the amount of time it will take to complete each to-do item; enter the figure alongside.
- Arrange the tasks in proper sequential order.
- Assign a completion date to each task and a target deadline for the entire project.

Make a Daily To-Do List

Prepare a to-do list *every* day. It's the favorite advice of time-management professionals. By preparing a daily list of things to do, you're ready to act when the time comes, with no need for further thought or preparation, no lost or wasted motion. You're always ready for action.

On your to-do list:

- Put down all the tasks you'd like to complete that day.
- Alongside each task, enter an estimate of how long it will take.

- Prioritize the list. First, put down the things that must be done in order of severity of consequence for failing; label these "A." Then put down the things you plan to get done; label them "B." Finally, put down the things you hope to get done; label them "C."
- Total the time-estimates for your "A" and "B" priorities. Make sure your day can accommodate all the assigned tasks. If not, reassess your priorities. Plan a reasonable day so you end it successfully by completing all the work you scheduled.

Salesman Gene McLemore kept his list on a computer in his office. "It was the first thing to pop up every morning," he says. As each chore was completed, he'd put a line of dashes through it, but he wouldn't delete the entry. "It was a perpetual list," he reveals with a chuckle.

What purpose did that serve? "If you erase the items on the list as they're completed, you're left with all the things you still have to do," McLemore explains. "It can be discouraging. Looking back at all the things I'd already accomplished always gave me a sense of satisfaction."

JUMP-START THE DAY

Need a motto to fight procrastination? Janet Burroway suggests the one hanging over her desk: "Don't Dread; Do."

Do whatever it takes.

Dorothy Lehmkuhl's slogan: "If it's to be, it's up to me."

Sue Hurlbut shares another well-known maxim: "Fail to plan, plan on failing."

Arriving at your desk ready and eager to work is critical stresses Hurlbut. Get there unfocused on what to do first, unsure of the direction you want your day to take, and chances are you'll never gain control.

"Seize the moment," she says, "or it will seize you."

Realtor Len Friedman, who's studying to be a lawyer on the side, rises at five each morning, not to read the paper or exercise but to sit and sip three successive cups of coffee in the gathering light of the new day.

In this quiet time, with nothing to distract him, he allows whatever thoughts, feelings, ideas, insights, or inspiration—whatever lies crouched on the rim of his consciousness and imagination—to coalesce into perception.

He mentally and emotionally stokes his engine for its impending ignition.

Gearing for Battle

"I sometimes wind up furiously scribbling snatches of copy," says Friedman. "Or I mentally stroll through a problem, consciously searching for answers. But mostly I just sit in the dark, letting my mind drift, waiting for the bulbs to click on.

"I troll for answers. Or I just energize myself for the moment when I sit down at my desk. It's the most important hour of my working day. It sets the mood and tone for everything to follow. I usually can't wait to get started!"

Helen Greer, who publishes a trade newsletter from home, spends a predawn hour on her exercise bike with a pad and pencil dangling from its handlebars to record her adrenaline-charged flashes of intuition. The inspiration comes with the sweat, assures Greer, and there's always plenty of both. She, too, is seldom at a loss for what to do when her working day starts.

Preparation Is Everything

Like Greer, Bob Griggs, a venture capitalist who operates out of his suburban home, greases the start of his working day with perspiration. He usually goes for an early morning run. It vitalizes him, he says. The thoughts and inspiration flow hot and heavy. He likens it to preparing a house for painting.

"The hard part's getting the structure ready," Griggs explains. "You don't just start splashing latex. First, there's furniture to be moved, drop cloths to be placed, masking tape to put down. I do all those things while I'm running. When I get to my desk, I'm ready to paint."

So don't plunk yourself down cold. Move the mental furniture around first. Get ready by warming up the brain cells, stretching your intellectual muscles. Be raring to go when the starting gun sounds.

WHAT TO DO WHEN YOU CAN'T GET GOING

There will be times, however, and they'll come, no matter how motivated or disciplined you are, when you simply *can't* get going, no matter how hard you try. When this happens, don't keep yourself lashed to the desk with guilt, chains, or whatever. Discretion here is the better part of valor.

When Elizabeth Donovan gets restless, she strolls to her piano and diverts herself with an etude or two.

"It's those day-to-day pleasures that make it all worthwhile," says the market researcher whose one-person firm is based in her Manhattan apartment. "I can take a break and walk over to Central Park, go take a dance class, or visit a museum."

The idea is to return rejuvenated, straining at the leash.

Never Surrender

But what if you get back to your desk and your diversionary tactic hasn't worked? You still can't bring yourself to work! Don't throw in the towel, at least not yet. Ask yourself first, "Can I compromise? If I can't save the day, can I at least salvage part of it?"

If you should be writing or finishing that report or rearranging the files or doing your taxes—whatever has you totally turned off—can you substitute other work instead? Will you settle for taking some research material or your reading file into the park? Or tackling those phone calls you'd put on hold until Thursday?

Always strike a deal with yourself. Come away from the bargaining table with something more than abject surrender.

Whenever you can't save the day, settle for a fragment of it, no matter how small. Consider it a moral victory. It will keep you from becoming a pushover in your 100-year war against procrastination.

Lose a Battle, Win the War

If something's on your mind, blocking you from what you ought to be doing and you can't disengage yourself from it, give in temporarily.

Lose the battle so you can return to the war.

Paul and Sarah Edwards recommend home-based publicist Kim Freilich-Dower's technique: "When she becomes distracted by her messy house, she stops working, sets a timer for 10 minutes and rushes to get as much housework done as she can before the timer goes off. When it rings, she goes back to work with her mind at ease."

Or check the TV guide. Is there a movie or sporting event or news program you'd like to see? Then make a deal with yourself: You'll watch the show, then complete that report, however long it takes. And if the game is boring, you'll turn it off and get back to work with a vengeance.

Remember, though, that reneging on your bargain turns compromise into procrastination. And the next time you want to make a deal, you won't trust the negotiator. Always be as good as your word. Flaking out on yourself can become an ugly habit.

Dissolving Writer's Block

Console yourself with the fact that most people experience mental constipation occasionally. Those of us who earn our living stringing words together call it writer's block. It's the chronic malady of our profession, and it's imperative that we unclog ourselves as quickly as possible. So we'll try anything, at least once.

Common tactics run the gamut of what other procrastinators try. "Writer's block" is a fancier name for goldbricking, probably dreamt up by a writer who was malingering at the time.

A favorite method for leveling writer's block consists of three little words: Lower your standards. With a second directive tacked on: Temporarily. Capped by a third: And get started!

How often do we never start something simply because we're afraid of failing? No problem. If you can't raise the confidence level, then lower the goal. At least temporarily. And get on with it.

It's all based on a positive attitude. That's the Draino of our psychic plumbing.

Relieve yourself of those negative thoughts. Replace them with positive feelings—some people call them "affirmations."

Use them like a mantra, a chant you intone over and over to ratchet you up emotionally, to develop the necessary attitude to achieve your goals.

"The first step," counsels *Writer's Digest* columnist Lawrence Block, "is getting out of your own way, and affirmations are as good a means toward that end as I know."

So go ahead, make your day.

If you can't, get a friend to help you. Unplugging resistance needn't be a solitary battle. Get yourself a crisis hotline. Recruit a mentor with an analytic eye and a sympathetic ear. Elicit his or her help when you're in trouble. Whenever you find yourself resisting a major task or stuck in a rut, phone your designated cheerleader.

Make it clear you might have to unburden yourself every hour on the hour until you're completely clear of whatever mental or emotional morass you've fallen into. And do just that—ventilate your concerns and frustrations as often as you like. Curse. Wail. Gnash your teeth. Complain to the high heavens. Get it all out. Sometimes you just have to hear yourself talk to figure out what's wrong.

Then treat your friend to a pizza and beer.

CHAPTER EIGHT

BEFRIENDING

SOLITUDE:

HOW TO BE ALONE,

NOT LONELY

Marge Foster could peddle ice to Eskimos. She sells just about everything else to others. Foster markets products by phone. It's called telemarketing. Dialing a quota of 50 to 60 prospects a day, wielding a charismatic voice, casual charm, and a keen sense of humor, she convinces enough people to buy whatever it is she's selling to earn a decent living without leaving home.

There was a time, however, when Foster desperately wanted to leave home.

Working alone had a devastating effect on the 34-year-old former secretary. In two years, she added 30 pounds to her diminutive frame. Her hunger, she finally figured out, was fueled by bouts with depression triggered by a sense of alienation. One fed voraciously on the other.

When she discovered loneliness was her real problem—not being too close to the refrigerator—she was on her way to righting herself.

"Dieting wasn't the answer," says Foster. "It was coping with my feeling of isolation. Once I realized that was what I had to beat, I was fine."

A brief smile, then: "It took me a while, but I now weigh close to what I did before I went solo. As I learned to handle my loneliness, I was able to control my eating. Taking care of one thing seemed to take care of the other."

Can You Handle Solitude?

Home alone with the job you love. It's the new American Dream. Unfortunately, it's the *alone* part many must learn to handle. Writer Ted Morgan puts it this way: "We yearn for Walden Pond, and forget that one can drown in Walden Pond."

Like Kearnes, some of us have to adjust accordingly. Others, like Cody and Simpson, compromise. For a fortunate few, solitude isn't a problem, it's a blessing. In fact, they can't get enough of it. If you're one of them, you're lucky.

Of all the obstacles to working alone, one towers above the rest—the psychological sumo wrestler of them all: Loneliness.

There's one question all marchers to their private drumbeats must ask themselves: Can I handle solitude?

Don't answer too quickly.

Throughout the ages, society has pounded into our collective consciousness the idea that no man is an island. And certainly no woman. From childhood we're conditioned to accept that alone, we instinctively ache for company. As teenagers we're rated by our circle of friends. As adults we're ranked, and we rank ourselves, by the quality of our personal and professional relationships.

We're taught that solitary confinement is, by its very nature, cruel and unusual punishment, the harshest possible discipline meted to convicts.

Little wonder, then, that society considers "sad" and "lonely," "alone" and "depressed," "separate" and "alienated" as synonymous emotional states in a nation that goes around in couples and crowds—not singly, and, if so, rarely by choice.

We accept instinctively that loners are geeks, weirdos, and outsiders yearning for company, rather than people who simply choose to be on their own.

Let's face it. It may be exhilarating and fulfilling being out there alone, but it's also scary. "Anxiety," said Søren Kierkegaard, "is the dizziness of freedom."

Can you handle it?

It's easier for some than others, depending on how much they need people. They may be the luckiest people in the word, as Barbra Streisand sings, but needing people when you choose to work alone can be a problem. And one you must address.

The Emotional Cost of Freedom

Barbara Powell, author of *Alone, Alive and Well*, offers some personal insight on the high emotional price that working alone exacts on some:

> Those who live alone should look carefully at the isolation. In the office where I sometimes work, various graphic artists have always worked at home and brought their results in to the office. The family men and women among them do what they need to do and rush away again; the single people hang around, sometimes for hours, trying to scratch up conversations.
>
> The human contact at the watercooler is not to be sneezed at. Psychologists hint that those of us who go through our days without faces and voices can easily go 'round the bend and start dressing like Napoleon or talking to pigeons. Solitary folk should be wary of such faceless, voiceless freedom. How shall we even end the working day? We turn off the computer and stand up, and we're still where we always were, and still alone.

"Yet it is essential to our souls," notes Sue Halpern in her contemplative book, *Migrations to Solitude*. Speaking for the millions of Americans who choose to be alone with their work, she asserts, "It is essential not only to the souls of painters and poets, who thrive in solitude, but to the rest of us, too—individuals whose canvas is our lives."

We just have to learn to live with it.

Making Your Own World

We who work alone must learn to "trust the silence," as Roger Rosenblatt puts it in an eloquent description of his 12-year-old son's enviable capacity to make his own world:

In a way I envy him his solitude. An adult so self-absorbed would be thought crazy, but for a child this time is creative. He gets to know himself as a separate entity, a close, yet mysterious friend who will remain with him all his life, like a muse or benevolent genie.

Children who spend a lot of time alone instill a special confidence in themselves. In part, this is because they always play the hero in their games. But it goes deeper.

In their solitude they find a room, in which they may touch their true and special nature, as in a cold, still pool of water hidden in the bottom of the earth. No one in their outer public life knows them as well as they are known in that room. No one imagines the peace, the poise and quiet courage they are capable of scooping up from the quality of their aloneness.

Some of us choose to color our canvasses in seclusion, others in a swirl of life. Still others find their creative comfort in a deliberate mix of both. Here, as in life itself, compromise is often essential.

WHAT TO DO WHEN THERE'S NO ONE BUT YOU

More than anything, Betsy Cluff misses people looking over her shoulder. She yearns for their input and feedback, even the occasional criticism. Now she must seek it when she thinks she needs it.

Being on her own has fostered a kind of insecurity, reveals the 41-year-old commercial artist, who has freelanced from her one-bedroom apartment for the past four years after being employed by commercial studios for eight years.

When she worked with peers, Cluff informs, wistfulness staining her voice, she received affirmation and reinforcement. Alone, she has become hypersensitive to her clients' reaction to her work. It is the only feedback she gets. When the response is less than she'd hoped for, her confidence and self-esteem can plummet. Then she has to handle the emotional letdown by herself.

Cluff does this in two ways. She reaffirms her self-worth, she says, by "programming" a success: "Doing something I'm very good at so that it invariably lifts my spirits." Or she challenges herself in some way. "I do it to expand my abilities," she says, "but also to calm my uncertainty and bolster my faith in myself."

Cluff perseveres in her solitary lifestyle for the control and creativity it fosters in her work. But she's yet to unravel the years of conditioning associated with "going to work," when she would travel to the office, have coffee with co-workers, then settle into the camaraderie of a familiar routine. Cluff still misses it.

"It was simple," she says, "something I just did. At home, I find it harder to get going. And ironically, to stay focused all by myself."

How to Nurture Yourself

One of the hardest lessons people on their own have to learn is that they are now both the giver and the receiver of everything they get. There's no one at their elbow to give them a helping hand. Understandably, for many home workers, being alone leads to a sense of alienation, from which springs loneliness unless they consciously work it out.

"What's important," says Cheryl Merser, author of *Grown Ups*, "is to fight isolation, no matter what one's living arrangements are. To face isolation is to face adult life."

There's a big difference between aloneness and isolation, points out Dean Ornish, an assistant clinical professor of medicine: "You can be alone by choice and not feel isolated. On the other hand, you can be the head of a large company, the center of your world, and still feel very isolated. By isolation, I mean not feeling a real sense of intimate connection with other people."

A strong sense of connectedness is critical to those who spend large portions of their working lives alone.

Tempering Solitude

The American high priest of solitude was Thoreau, Barbara Holland acknowledges in her book, *One's Company: Reflections on Living Alone.* "We admire him," she writes, "not for his self-reliance and his conceited musings, but because he was all by himself out there at Walden Pond, and he *wanted* to be. All alone in the *woods*."

But he lived a mile, or 20 minutes' walk, from his nearest neighbor, half a mile from the railroad, three hundred yards from a busy highway, Holland points out. "He had streams of company in and out of the hut all day, asking him how he could possibly be so noble," she says, tweaking the high priest's celebrated conceit.

"Thoreau had his own self-importance for company. Thoreau alone with Thoreau was a crowd. Perhaps there's a message here," Holland concludes: "The larger the ego, the less the need for other egos around. The more modest, humble, and self-effacing we feel, the more we suffer from solitude, feeling ourselves inadequate company."

How large is *your* ego? Big enough to allow you to be at home with yourself? Or do you need periodic doses of other people? Think about it.

CREATIVE SOLUTIONS:
ALONE IN THE COMPANY OF OTHERS

To work alone, John Kearnes must retreat into a crowd.

At home, he says, the silence is deafening, the feeling of isolation overpowering. He needs people around him.

He is a loner by nature, and by choice, he readily admits. But the 37-year-old house appraiser is also a lonely person and knows he must temper his voluntary seclusion with the company of others in order to function productively.

So he works with a pad, pencil, and pocket adding machine, swaddled by the sights and sounds—the comfort—of human activity. In restaurants, coffee shops and libraries, on park benches and lawns, varying his routine and public haunts with the seasons and the daily weather.

It's what he must do, he says, to survive professionally.

Novelist Robin Cody also likes having people around when he works—for half his day, at least.

The 53-year-old Portland, Oregon author of *Ricochet River* has a singular routine. He's up at first light, eats a breakfast of fruit and granola, then mounts his 10-speed bike for an adrenaline-pumping ride to a fast-food restaurant, usually a McDonald's or Burger King, some 45 minutes' pedaling distance from his house.

Here, he commandeers a table for three to four hours and pens his first drafts on tablet paper.

Enter the Portable Office

Why not a quieter place with better coffee? "The turnover's so rapid, no one notices or cares whether you hog a table all morning," Cody replies. Nonetheless, he shifts his portable office periodically so he doesn't become a fixture in any one place.

Why not just stay home? Cody shrugs. "It feels good to have people around me. I don't have a problem with being alone. I'm happily married and have an active social life, so it has nothing to do with filling a void in my life. It's just how I like to work."

He's usually back on his bike by 11:30, he says, before the lunch crowd drifts in. The ride home is an energizing break. Then he rounds off the day in his office, a 15' x 20' space off the master bedroom. Here, hemmed in by books and computer equipment instead of people, he electronically records the copy he scribbled in longhand at the restaurant.

"It's mornings out, afternoons in," Cody says with a grin. "That way, one place or the other doesn't get to me. It's a change of pace as well as scenery."

Nomadic Workers

Very much like Robin Cody, novelist Mona Simpson, author of *Anywhere But Here* and its sequel, *The Lost Father*, is a nomadic worker, doing much of her writing on the run, scribbling in notebooks in public places such as bustling restaurants and cafes.

"I do my best work at concerts," she insists, "when I'm stuck for the duration." She has used a different rented office for each of her novels, growing "sick" of the space as her work is done and moving to another for her next project.

New York author Marissa Piesman writes her books on the subway. She averages 400 words per 50-minute ride, scribbling her words on a stenographic pad. That's 4,000 words a week. In nine months she has the rough draft of another novel. She's written three of them while taking the "A" train, undistracted by the press of humanity around her or the conductor's repeated pleas to watch the closing doors.

FACING YOUR LONELINESS

There's much to learn about combatting loneliness. But first, if you're to acknowledge the adversary you dread most and must tame, it helps to understand the nature of the beast itself.

Those who tend to be lonely need to accept the feeling as natural, not something to be denied. Understand that we're all social creatures by nature, that a sense of belonging to others is basic to a sense of self.

"Don't underestimate how much of your identity comes from interacting with other people," cautions marketing consultant Marcia Hoyt. "If I spend enough time alone, I start looking in the mirror and asking myself, 'Who am I?' Brushing up against others gives me a sense of what I'm all about."

Hoyt knows she has to compensate for being alone. "I need situations with lots of emotional support," she says. "I need a close, nurturing community of co-workers and friends. Otherwise, I know I'd become like those touch-deprived infants you read about who shrivel up from lack of human contact.

"We have to make sure we have something other than ourselves to draw from," Hoyt concludes. "Otherwise, we stunt our growth, emotionally as well as intellectually." And, of course, professionally.

Recognizing the Triggers of Loneliness and the Benefits of Being On Your Own

Know, too, that loneliness can be triggered by many things. Altered social situations, such as divorce or separation, can bring it on. Or the death of a loved one. Or the move to a new community. Or the start of a new job or career. Or change itself can do it.

What's more, a variety of personal traits such as introversion, shyness, and low self-esteem make certain individuals more vulnerable to loneliness than others. As a result of these personal and situational variables, there are those among us who feel lonely occasionally. Others are chronically lonely, while still others seldom or never feel lonely.

Yet, loneliness isn't the worst feeling in the world. We think it is because we've been conditioned to regard aloneness as a generally undesirable state. But that's changing as more and more people in an increasingly chaotic world are finding solitude to be a pleasant, stimulating, enlightening, and highly desirable place.

Hold that thought. Nurture that feeling.

Remind yourself: I'm alone because I've chosen to be alone. I'm alone because my work allows me to be independent. I'm alone because of my passion for what I do for a living, and how well I do it centers and sustains me. It affirms who and what I am. It validates my existence. Being alone is an integral part of who I am.

Understandably, therefore, most creative activities are predominantly solitary, concerned primarily with self-realization and self-development. "The degree," writes Anthony Storr, eloquent author of *Solitude: A Return to the Self*, "to which these creative activities take priority in the life of an individual varies with his personality and talents.

"Everyone needs some human relationships; but everyone also needs some kind of fulfillment which is relevant to himself alone."

HOW TO HANDLE THE TRANSITION TO WORKING ALONE

Suddenly and traumatically discharged from a local firm she'd help build into a multistate operation, Sue Hurlbut found herself with nothing to do and extremely depressed. Her two home-based companies, Organization Plus and HTO Enterprises resulted.

She started the first business to allay her depression, "like grabbing someone on the rebound after a failed personal relationship," she says. Though the venture was an immediate success, she struggled with working alone.

"One of the things that bothered me most as a corporate manager was having to deal with constant interruptions," Hurlbut relates. "I'd long thought of myself as ideally suited to being completely on my own. I'm a self-starter who accomplishes things in long bursts of concentrated activity, and the prospect of doing it without being interrupted seemed highly appealing."

Yet she soon discovered, to her great surprise, that she sorely missed the daily interaction with co-workers. She found herself constantly leaving the office to chat with neighbors. "I was forever making deals with myself to postpone working until the evening so I could enjoy the sun, run errands, or see a movie."

She rationalized it made no difference whatsoever to anyone else when she did her work, yet she knew in her heart she was shirking her work because she craved the company of other people.

Share the Bad Stuff

Single, with her family scattered around the country, Hurlbut found the worst part of being on her own was not having anyone to readily share "the bad stuff" in her life—the irregular income and financial worries of running her own business, how hard it all gets sometimes.

"It's easy to pick up the phone and talk about the good things that happen to you," she points out. "But you carry around the sense that if you tell people you're having trouble, their perception of your ability to succeed will be diminished."

She belongs to a number of organizations, several of them extremely supportive of entrepreneurs like herself. But she feels she has to be unrelentingly upbeat with the other members.

"They're also potential clients and referral sources," Hurlbut reasons. "Would they hire or recommend me if they weren't sure I was capable of succeeding?" Hurlbut asks herself.

"Who's it safe to share the bad stuff with? Who's even willing to listen and able to provide objective feedback?"

What's the answer?

Necessary Growth

"You have to trust people," she replies. "It's that simple. Everyone's alone. People on their own just realize it a lot sooner. We're all struggling. We all have the same hopes and fears, the same needs, and unless we reach out to each other, we really will be isolated and lonely."

Hurlbut feels that if her businesses failed tomorrow, the exponential personal growth that's come from being on her own will have made it all worthwhile. "I'm a very different person now," she says.

"People usually start a company because they're good at doing or making something. But that's only half the battle. I was good with paperwork, devising budgets, creating business plans, that sort of thing.

"But I was a total wallflower. I rarely spoke up or expressed my opinion. I didn't make eye contact or assert myself in any way. I was totally passive and reactive, never proactive, in all my personal and business relationships."

That's all changed, Hurlbut asserts triumphantly. "Being on your own means counting only on yourself for everything it takes to succeed. It forces you to become O. K. by yourself because you have to.

"It makes you take risks you'd never have taken otherwise. It teaches you about yourself and turns you from being lonely and scared to being alone and strong."

USING SOLITUDE WELL

Barbara Powell, author of *Alone, Alive and Well*, agrees that the best way to conquer loneliness is to know yourself so well—the things you enjoy and the things you don't, what gives you a feeling of accomplishment and well-being—that when you're alone, the time isn't empty because of what you choose to do with it.

Only people who can *use* solitude, not constantly battle it, are free to fully explore their thoughts and feelings, to develop an identity based on a real and intimate knowledge of themselves, says Powell.

That secure, intimate knowledge of self is essential to being on your own.

However you confront the spectre of loneliness, know that it will stalk your electronic cottage. Know you may have to exorcise it occasionally, but don't fear this gray ghost of your solitude.

It could become the best friend you ever had.

How To Be Alone, Not Lonely

1. *Stay connected with others.* Use your daily contacts with family, friends, professional peers, and business associates to maintain a feeling of intimacy with other people.

If you can't be all things to yourself, count on others to help protect you from the unreasonable doubts and fears that will rise to the surface of your solitude. Seek others to energize you, to help you believe that you and what you're doing are worthwhile and important.

Others is the operative word here. Many of us can only bear to be alone if firmly connected to others, as if by a deep-sea diver's lifeline or in a sturdy shark cage. Only then, assured we're firmly connected and can pull ourselves back up to emotional safety, are we willing to descend into the murky depths of our own company. Knowing this about ourselves, we must make a conscious, deliberate effort to stay firmly tethered to others:

2. *Schedule a breakfast meeting.* Or lunch or dinner. Do it often.

3. *Make a personal phone call* once in a while. Encourage family, friends, and business associates to call so the phone rings regularly.

4. *Chat electronically* on national computer networks. An increasing number of home workers are using this prolific medium to "converse" with others who have similar interests. It's a great way to stave off a sense of isolation.

Do some computer schoozing. Use the Internet, a giant party line for electronic communicators, many of whom work from their homes. The Internet can be reached through a number of information services such as America Online and CompuServe.

Computer electronic mail—e-mail to the computer intelligentsia—is a broad, deep pool of fascinating information sources. You can use electronic mail to share data, record phone messages, make dates, converse with kindred, disembodied spirits, and swap quips and phone numbers. And you don't even have to dress up to make a good impression.

5. *Get out of the office regularly.* Have that midafternoon coffee in a restaurant instead of your kitchen. Work out at the health club—exercise your mouth along with your muscles. Go for a walk or a run or a bike ride. Buy a book or some flowers. Visit a friend. Whatever takes you outside—the office and yourself—for awhile. Make it a natural part of your daily routine so you won't feel the crushing need for it.

6. *Find a great good place.* In his marvelous book, *The Great Good Place*, they're what Ray Oldenburg calls "hospitable institutions of mediation between the individual and larger society": A *Cheers* bar, a yogurt shop, or a neighborhood diner where everybody knows your name.

Elsewhere in the world these great good places take the welcoming form of Parisian cafes, Italian piazzas, Viennese coffeehouses, English pubs, German beer gardens, and Japanese teahouses. They help keep our proud independence from becoming pitiable isolation.

Deprived of great good places that nourish human contact, people on their own risk an increasing sense of alienation. Visit your own great good place once in a while. Be with others, if only for a while.

7. *Get a pet.* Dave Barry's two dogs keep him company while he works, he tells us in a column he did on how much he enjoys working from home. Earnest ("named for his sincerity") likes to lie under his desk and bark occasionally. Zippy hangs around waiting for errant scraps of the four peanut butter (and no jelly) sandwiches the syndicated columnist diverts himself with each working day. Barry likes having the dogs around, and that's reason enough.

Janet Livesay's 14-year-old weimaraner, Dolly, makes the daily commute to Livesay's one-person office, where she snoozes on a throw rug at Livesay's feet. "She calms me down," says the printing broker. "And I have to walk her regularly, which gets me outside and provides an outlet for my nervous energy."

Marketing consultant Sarah Gates credits her dog and two cats with helping her through the interminable stretches of studying alone at home when she was in graduate school.

Feeling more and more alone while spending a winter in an old Vermont farmhouse, novelist Joseph Olshan borrowed one of his friend's dogs to soften his isolation. "Because their emotions are so pure," Olshan later wrote, "dogs can often touch the deepest part of us. And in so doing they might in their own way prepare us to understand ourselves."

So next time you feel angry or upset, depressed or lonely, count to 10 and pet the dog or cat, or your potbellied pig, or cockatoo, or the newest exotic pet, a hedgehog. Then both of you go for a walk together.

8. *Tell yourself: This too will pass.* A sure way to feel emotional isolation is to become so immersed in your work that you believe there's no time for anyone or anything else. Recalling a period in her life in which she pursued an M.B.A. while running a one-person horticultural business, Julie Stream's face clouds over. "I was constantly overwhelmed," the 41-year-old pharmaceutical representative recounts with a frown.

"I was always anxious about getting it all done and fearful I wouldn't, always pressured and struggling, always pushing to make maximum use of my time. There was no time for handholding, no room for friends or a social life. I felt alienated, terribly lonely. I can still feel the loneliness," she says, "right here," patting the pit of her stomach.

How did she get through it? "More than anything," Stream replies, "it was the fear of failure that helped me handle the self-imposed isolation and loneliness. My need to succeed helped me gut it out. I know now that loneliness passes. So does self-doubt and being so bone-deep weary you think you're going to feel that way forever.

"I learned it's even O. K. to feel sorry for yourself once in a while, to cry and tell yourself, 'I'm so sick of this!' as long as you hang in there. Because it *will* pass. And one day you'll be left with what you worked so hard to achieve. The rest will fade away."

9. *Be good to yourself.* Be a taskmaster, but an appreciative one. Work hard, but reward yourself generously. Unremitting tedium does, indeed, lead to emotional isolation and burnout. An office in the home should allow ample time to intersperse toil with remuneration. Indulge yourself. Who says you can't? Or shouldn't? Both your mind and body can use the breaks. Just don't overdo them.

Take a nap. See a movie. Ride your bike. Go for a run. Call your mother. Read a book. Watch your favorite soap opera or talk show on TV. Fix yourself a midafternoon hamburger. Listen to music while doing nothing else.

"Forget for a while about exercising good time-management," urges psychologist Al Siebert. "Forget about being productive for awhile. "Forget about shining your shoes, writing letters, or cleaning out your desk. Just sit back and lose yourself in the music. The very word stems from the act of musing. Do it. Muse."

Take time to meditate, says Siebert, an expert on survival behavior. "Let your mind wander. Or go blank. Don't use every free moment to think through your problems. Forget what's bothering you occasionally and just let yourself feel good. Focus your attention on a lovely, tranquil scene. Recall a particularly pleasant experience. Take relaxing breaths. Find out what it means to get centered."

Remember, as a person working alone you don't have to conform to anyone else's schedule, standards, or expectations. You can work all night Friday, all day Saturday and Sunday, knowing that when you're past the big push you can make it up to yourself.

Be good to yourself, regularly and often.

"It's important to be self-nourishing," says Siebert. "Don't confuse self-nourishment with selfishness. Psychologically healthy people are both selfish and unselfish. They act in ways that are beneficial to their own well-being while still being helpful to others.

"They recognize that they can't be good to others unless they're good to themselves."

10. *Look on the bright side.* Work at being pleasant, optimistic, and positive. Not only is it essential to your emotional well-

being as a solitary worker but your physical health may depend on it. Studies show that constantly angry, cynical, and aggressive individuals are coronary-prone.

Observes Philadelphia journalist Laura Masnerus: "If every negative emotion given a name—fear, depression, loneliness, dread, anxiety, resentment, and more—sets in motion some physiological disturbance, it cannot bode well for those chronically afflicted by any of them."

A new study by State University of New York researchers shows that the biggest setbacks to human immune systems are caused by work friction—particularly criticism by one's supervisor, by frustrating or irritating encounters with co-workers, and by the pressures of looming deadlines and heavy workloads.

By choosing to work alone, you've eliminated half those potential setbacks. You can banish the other half with a sunny disposition. Be kind to yourself and your immune system. Increase your daily dose of fun and friends, social activities and other leisure pursuits. Wrap yourself in a positive attitude, particularly when you're alone. Don't tell yourself it doesn't matter because you're alone: Your mind and body know better.

11. *Enjoy your own company.* Learn to like yourself. Spending as much time as you do alone, with so much time to think, it's imperative your thoughts be kind, especially about yourself. Relish the pleasure of your own company and you'll look forward to being with yourself, perhaps as often as possible. If not, you'll probably dislike and resent this unfortunate individual trapped in your skin. Face it: Since you're stuck with each other, you may as well become a beautiful couple. Beautiful couples are seldom lonely.

12. *Like your office.* Because you spend so much time in it alone, it's imperative you enjoy being there. If it's a place you really don't like, you're probably going to avoid having to go there—and feel lonely when you're forced to.

"We work at home," Erica Jong points out in a *New York Times* article, "indulging the agoraphobia endemic to our kind. We are immersed in our surroundings to an almost morbid degree. Not only do we see terrifying apparitions that the rest of our families miss, but we sometimes hear loud whispers and feel unearthly chills on our backs."

Maybe it's not quite that bad with you, but it *is* expedient to your success—and to befriending your solitude—that you make where you work a warm and friendly environment. Do whatever you have to, including finding a new office, to make it an appealing, inviting, productive place. It should exist, as Jong says, "to be a steward of our dreams." If it is, chances are you won't be lonely there.

13. *Have a company picnic.* "We who work alone can't look forward to a company picnic," sympathizes survival expert Al Siebert. "It would be pretty lonely. How would we pick a softball team? Who would we run the three-legged race with? There are many emotional benefits to working alone, but there's the isolation to contend with.

"Have your company picnic anyway," he urges. "Get together with others like yourself. It's important to be with people with whom you have some history, who know and like you. It's one of the best antidotes for loneliness."

14. *Talk to yourself.* "One of the joys of working from home," points out guided imagery expert Patricia Megan Pingree, "is escaping from the 'down' side of working with others—the interruptions, the office gossip and personality conflicts, the mismatches of style and pace. Paradoxically, however, that same escape from others can bring its own set of stressors—the loss of positive feedback, the absence of a sympathetic ear and a ready shoulder to cry on, a withdrawal from the chitchat of coffee breaks. The result can be loneliness."

Yet the symptoms of loneliness may be difficult to trace to their source, says Pingree. "We may feel depressed or anxious or vaguely uneasy without realizing the cause is that we're simply not getting enough of the right kind of human contact."

Confusing the issue, she adds, is the fact that the 'right kind' of contact, at the right time, in the right amount, varies tremendously from person to person. "Some experience aloneness as life-enriching solitude, a treasured time to concentrate, to recharge internal batteries. For others, aloneness is uncomfortable, anxiety-producing, and depressing.

"'What's wrong with me?' the latter individual might ask. 'MaryBeth doesn't talk to anyone all week and she loves it! A day by myself and I'm climbing the walls!' When you feel that way, it's a good time to remember to have a nurturing talk with yourself," advises Pingree.

"Berating yourself for how you feel will only make you feel worse. Your own needs are unique and valid to you, so you may as well learn what they are and how to meet them. And an excellent way to find out is by having regular chats with yourself. Only you can tell yourself what aspects of aloneness make you feel lonely."

Talk Out Loud If It Helps

PR consultant Joleen Colombo readily admits she talks to herself—often and out loud—but not in company, she demurs. "It helps me when I'm feeling very much alone. I have these incredible conversations with myself, sometimes laughing, sometimes applauding my success, sometmes shouting how good I feel." A pause. "But I don't answer myself," she adds.

Talking out loud also helps Colombo figure things out. Sometimes she rehearses what she plans to say in critical situations. Sometimes she expresses whatever anger, disappointment, frustration, confusion, or doubt she might be experiencing. If there's someone responsible for those negative feelings, she imagines that person in the room with her and talks things over. "When I hear only my side," she explains, "I realize my point-of-view is one-dimensional, and I start seeing the other person's side.

"Talking out loud to yourself can be tremendously therapeutic," Colombo claims. "It's a marvelous way to work through negative emotions without doing anyone else harm. I heartily recommend it to everyone who works alone. In a void of silence, with only a forum of one, your voice can be a healing, instructive, and comforting instrument."

Talk things over with yourself regularly, also urges Pingree. Ask: Which features of aloneness appeal to me and which don't? Which feel like solitude, which like loneliness? How can I enhance the experience of aloneness so that it nourishes me? How can I minimize my loneliness?

"Ask the questions," she says," and the answers will come."

Engage in Active Solitude

Keep in mind, however, that the ways we tend to relieve loneliness—phone breaks, lunches with friends, social contacts, great good places, and other pleasurable diversions—are basically *retreats* from solitude. They are effective in varying degrees and certainly necessary at times. But they are also nonproductive methods of coping, from the standpoint of getting your work done.

Be clear in your mind between an *excuse* not to work and a valid *reason* for not working.

A survey by Carin Rubenstein and Phillip Shaver yielded diverse responses to the question, "When you feel lonely, what do you usually do about it?" Respondents' reactions ranged from crying and napping to writing, working, and phoning friends. The responses were grouped into four categories: *sad passivity* (doing nothing, sleeping, thinking), *active solitude* (writing, exercising, working), *social contact* (phoning or visiting with a friend), and *shopping*.

The point is, there are many ways to remedy the occasional cabin fever that may grip you as a home worker. Instead of retreating from loneliness, however, can you respond to it by devoting even more verve and dedication to your work? If so, active solitude will prove not only therapeutic but productive as well.

Hold Your Ground

Writer's Digest columnist Art Spikol surrounds himself with photos of loved ones. Tacked to his computer are pictures of his daughters. They remind him of "what life is all about," he says. "Sanctuary though it may be, there will be times when you wish you didn't have to be in that office. After looking at them for a minute or so, I can go back to work."

For me, taking a few minutes off to pay some bills, particularly the mortgage, provides the same kind of stimulus.

Fending off feelings of isolation, as author Cheryl Merser points out, is critical to survival. To fight isolation is to face adult life—and crucial to being on your own.

And the testing grounds are your mind and heart. For being alone is not the same as being isolated unless you mentally make that equation. Being on your own means being alone. It doesn't mean being lonely. Unless you let it.

THE IDEAL HOME OFFICE: PERSONAL FIT IS EVERYTHING

Offices are like clothes. Tailor-made beats off-the-rack any day of the week.

"Fit is everything," confirms professional organizer Sue Hurlbut. "Looks are important, but how well your working environment suits you is critical to your productivity."

CREATING THE IDEAL HOME OFFICE

People who set up a home office have a real tendency to "make do," she cautions. "And creating an ideal working environment involves tailoring the space to the individual who occupies it. Not investing the necessary thought and effort to make a suitable match is like having a friend find a spouse for you because you can't be bothered."

Questions to Ask Yourself

Begin by visualizing what kind of activities will take place in your office before settling on a work space, Hurlbut advises. Decide

123

what furniture and equipment—specifically what kind of *environment*—will meet your needs. Anticipate how those requirements may change in the next few years. Ask yourself:

WHAT KIND OF IMAGE, IF ANY, AM I TRYING TO CONVEY? Will clients be visiting me in my office? If so, will the setting be appropriate? Do I need a conference room as well as an office? Does the conference area have to be exclusive or can it be shared with other tenants or members of the family?

How important is the impression my office makes on others? Does it matter where I work as long as I'm productive there, or is an upscale office in a professional building vital to my success?

Is it vital I impress potential clients with my mailing address? Will a post office box in any area of town suffice? Or will a P. O. box number telegraph the fact that I'm working from home? If so, does it matter? (To disguise the fact that his office is situated in his suburban residence, one marketing consultant identifies it as "Suite 300" on his mailing address.)

IS THE OFFICE SUITED TO MY WORK? Do I need solitude? A "creative" environment? Will I be content to be in the office for long periods of time—comfortable, motivated, and productive while I'm there?

Is my work contemplative or administrative in nature? Is it service, production, or shipping oriented? Is there adequate room for the functions that will take place there? Will there be enough unloading, warehousing, or storage space? Exactly what kind of equipment and furniture will I need? Is there enough room to accommodate it?

Is the wiring adequate? Are there enough electrical outlets? Am I going to be too warm in the summer, too cold in winter? Am I setting up a permanent or temporary office? Will I soon outgrow the space physically or emotionally? Do I anticipate hiring part-time or full-time employees? What then?

IS THE LIGHTING SUITABLE? Typical corporate workplaces offer balanced, overhead lighting that spreads a pervasive bright-white light conducive to reading and working. Appropriate lighting directly affects productivity and adds to employees' energy levels by closely approximating sunlight.

Home offices, on the other hand, are typically illuminated by desk and floor lamps with incandescent bulbs that cast a yellow glow in limited areas, usually creating large pools of shadow and leaving most of the room dim. The mind recognizes this kind of lighting as "cozy" and "relaxed." Trouble is, the subconscious should be registering "action" and "activity."

Soft lighting, therefore, may adversely influence your overall sense of professionalism. Desk lamps with yellow incandescent or even fluorescent lighting may be inadequate for prolonged reading, leading to headaches and eyestrain.

So pay proper attention to the lighting in your home office.

WHAT ABOUT NATURAL LIGHT? Essential to painters and other artists, natural light is an appealing source of illumination and will influence the amount of artificial light you'll need in your work space. But ask yourself: Is it a consistent source of light? Will I have to block it out for a large portion of the day because too much heat or glare will result from the direct sunlight? Where should I place my desk, table, or work-station in relation to the natural light?

A skylight can, indeed, produce too much heat and glare, so it shouldn't be directly over your desk. Windows behind your desk create shadows, so natural light should come from the front or side. Easterly windows receive too much light in the morning. Windows on the west get too much light in the afternoon. Windows with a southern exposure get too much light most of the day.

That leaves windows facing north. These are the best source of natural light because they don't receive direct sun but offer sufficient daylight.

WILL A WINDOW DISTRACT ME? Is a view of the outside world disruptive to your concentration? Would an enclosed, womb-like atmosphere be more conducive to your creativity? Are the windows into your soul the only ones you care to peer through?

For some, however, the airy, spacious feeling that windows provide is essential to their psychic well-being.

As with most everything, the answer lies in a working balance, not only between natural and fluorescent light but also between practical, esthetic, and financial considerations. Yet the owner of an office in the home may not care to install "institutional" overhead lighting regardless of how beneficial it may be to his work.

In this case, the answer may be fluorescent light fixtures made of wood rather than metal, equipped with special tubes that soften the light, reduce glare, and are more pleasing to the eye in more ways than one. Naturally, cost considerations come into play here. Despite the added expense, however, some people will want to invest in full-spectrum lighting, which is also available in fluorescent varieties.

For those homeworkers who feel deprived of sunlight because of being indoors so much of the time, or who suffer from Seasonal Affective Disorder (SAD), full-spectrum lighting is a necessary expenditure in illuminating the workplace. Incandescent and ordinary fluorescent lighting lack portions of the light spectrum that are significant to the well-being of both plant and animal life, claims Jacob Liberman, author of *Light, Medicine of the Future.*

The bottom line on office lighting is that it must provide adequate illumination, cast minimal shadows on the work surface, and be bright enough to stimulate you to action rather than lull you into relaxation. Beyond optimum eye comfort, which is essential to sustained productivity, it's up to you to reach your own comfort level in that no-man's (or no-woman's) land between esthetics and cost, between beauty and function.

WHAT KIND OF FURNITURE DO I NEED? Proper furniture is *extremely* important. Especially your chair. If you can't afford anything else, invest in a good chair. Get one that's adjustable, has enough padding on the seat and back to allow for comfort, yet encourages proper posture by allowing you to sit with your feet flat on the floor and slightly apart.

You should be able to adjust the height and tilt of both the chair seat and back, as well as the distance of the seat from its back. A prolonged "slump" can wreak as much havoc on an office worker's lower back as on a baseball player's batting average.

If the chair puts your legs to sleep or causes you back pain, shoulder strain, or other such discomforts, replace it as soon as possible. And offer clients who come to your office the same consideration you accord yourself, namely a chair that allows them to concentrate on what is being said and done instead of what their bodies are feeling.

WHAT KIND OF DESK? There's an incredible array of desks in the marketplace, from roll-top antiques to modular slabs with a top, supports, and nothing else. The desk that's right for you depends entirely on what your work requires.

Here especially, function dictates form.

If what you do is artistic or creative in nature—or if you're a sensitive, visually discriminating individual, highly responsive to your working environment—aesthetic appeal assumes a large part of function.

If it's sheer working room you need and you couldn't care less what form it takes, there's your answer. The needed work area is the determining factor. Ask yourself what kinds of things you like to keep close to you, either on top of the desk or in the drawers, and make sure your desk provides that amount of space.

A rule of thumb for the minimum "active" area you need is indicated by the sweep of your extended arm while you're seated at the desk. This needs to be empty space, available for ongoing projects. So there should be enough room elsewhere on the desk to accommodate other items such as framed photos, plants, and lamps.

WHAT OTHER OFFICE FURNITURE DO I NEED? Because we live in an information age but haven't become comfortable with electronic storage, the traditional option consists of makeshift crates and boxes or traditional file cabinets. When choosing a file cabinet, make sure it affords easy access to all the drawer space.

Some cabinets have stops that prevent the drawers from being pulled all the way out, which can make it difficult for you to get into the files at the back. Check the depth of the drawers as well; some are only 15″ deep, others 18″, still others 22″. Each inch of space means two to five additional file folders you can store.

What about standard-size vs. legal-size cabinets, file folders, and supplies? Going the latter route costs more money and uses more floor space. Is it worth the additional investment? Apply the "two-thirds rule." If up to two-thirds of your documents and materials are legal-sized, the answer is clear. If not, legal-sized papers can be folded into letter-sized folders. Just don't make it too hard on yourself.

You'll probably also need shelving space for books and supplies. To accommodate these materials, use as much wall space as possible, making sure you attach the shelves and wall units with fasteners capable of sustaining the weight loads. Place stacker baskets on bookshelves for additional space. Think vertically. Store upward rather than sideways.

Are Right-Brain and Left-Brain Considerations Important in Selecting Office Furniture?

Very much so, particularly as regards filing systems, instructs Dorothy Lehmkuhl, co-author of *Organizing for the Creative Person*. Right- or left-brain dominance should dictate the size and type of your working surface, as well as how your files and materials are stored and displayed.

Because right-brain people are creative, visually-oriented types with random thinking patterns, they tend to favor bigger desk tops. The reason is that *seeing* things—shapes, patterns, colors, textures—provides them with mental and emotional stimulation. In fact, they may prefer tables and countertops to traditional desks, as well as horizontal, open-face storage bins such as stacker baskets to file drawers.

In addition, right-brain people tend to be "immediate" in that they want everything in direct view, preferring not to have to rummage through drawers and dig into file folders to find what they need. Nor do they want to go through the same process when putting papers away.

Poet Alexandra Kristall, who works from a compact one-bedroom apartment, suggests using large mailing envelopes stored *vertically*, however. Identify each folder by writing on the left side of the flap with a broad felt-tip marker. These giant "labels" assure easy identification of each envelope's contents, making the file system highly accessible—an important consideration for right-brain people, she reasons. Items can be readily deposited into the open-ended envelopes. What's more, an assortment of colored envelopes used in tandem with felt-tip markers of various vivid colors can provide a highly visual, efficient method of classifying the various file contents.

Kristall also touts straw baskets as excellent, eye-pleasing organizers. Put the desk items you use most in one basket, she instructs, the items you use less frequently in another, and the items you use only occasionally in a third basket. Keep the priority basket within easiest reach, and drop used staples into it. Each time you dump out the staple collection, you can reevaluate whether the items in that basket are, in fact, the ones you need at your fingertips.

Right-brain people also have an innate fear that if something isn't in plain view, it will be lost forever in an anonymous file drawer. Out of sight is literally out of mind, an uneasy feeling for them. Logical thinking can, of course, overcome their irrational unease, but they possess a very real need to have everything in plain sight, says Lehmkuhl.

Understandably, then, creative individuals are usually more comfortable working at a table—the bigger the better—because being able to see all their "stuff" helps them to be at their best. If you're such an individual, get a large table (more than 30" deep) so you can store your items in containers and bins at the rear of the table, rather than in desk drawers.

Again, be sure to leave an open area encompassed by the sweep of your arm as an active workspace. Along with providing adequate workspace, the table (or desk) must be able to accommodate all the items required for your current work, including all the papers and information you refer to daily. If your work is paper-intensive, you may want an inordinately large table. Or more than one.

It is most important that right-brain people set up their offices so they'll be totally at ease in them, instead of arbitrarily conforming to someone else's standards. Feelings of comfort, familiarity, and relaxation are an important part of the creative process.

In contrast, people with dominant left brains are highly logical folks who reason linearly, Lehmkuhl points out. They prefer large drawers, and lots of them, because they like to put away whatever they're not working on. Because of their operating style, they may need a credenza as well as a desk for extra storage. And they prefer to file their material in folders, placed vertically in drawers.

Obviously, individuals with more or less equal right-brain and left-brain capacity are comfortable with a balance of both sets of requirements. These people tend to favor standard 30″ x 60″ desks, generally equipped with three to five standard drawers, preferring to stash their current documents in file folders in these drawers.

Chances are that one or more of three limiting factors will come into play in your search for an ideal table or desk: Money, space, and time. Here are some options for coping. If the limitation is:

1. *Money.* Prioritize your needs. Shop for used furniture. Lease or rent what you need. Barter or trade.

2. *Space.* Consider several smaller items rather than one large piece. Look for furniture with multiple uses. Consider store-away products that fold compactly or can be moved out of sight or reach when not in use.

3. *Time.* Shop through catalogs. Visit stores that carry a full range of furniture, office equipment, and supplies. Consider only fully assembled products.

Quick Tips for Designing a Home Office on a Limited Budget

- A sheet of plywood or pressboard supported by a couple of two-drawer file cabinets makes an inexpensive and functional desk.

- A pull-out drawer or two added to any kind of shelving effectively creates storage space.

- Stacker baskets on shelves serve the same functional purpose of multiplying usable space.

- A cookbook stand on the desk can hold your day-planner upright, in clear view and easy reach while taking up much less desktop space than if it were spread flat.

- Phone books (or other softcover books used frequently) can be stored flat on a side shelf below desktop level.

BEFORE YOU BUY CHECKLIST

Sketch everything out in your mind and on paper beforehand. Look through catalogs and in stores. Weigh all your options and price them competitively.

Remember, you'll be spending more time at work than at home—most of it seated in your chair, at your desk—so don't "outgrow" your furniture too quickly. Balance frugality, on one hand, with buyer's remorse, on the other, over not having invested enough to secure exactly what you need and want.

Before you whip out the old credit card, determine your precise requirements—physical, emotional, and aesthetic. This exercise will help you make smart buys:

1. *List your tasks*: What kinds of activity will your work take, presently and in the near future?

2. *List your "tools:"* Exactly what furniture and equipment will you need to accomplish those tasks? Put everything down that you can think of.

3. *Cross off everything you already have that will do the job*. But delete only the items that are satisfactory to you. Keep the ones you'd replace if you could.

4. *The rest becomes your shopping list*. Before you set out, though, know where to go to find what you need.

WHAT ABOUT TELEPHONES? Is there much to think about in this regard? The answer is an emphatic *yes!* Ask yourself:

1. *Do I need more than one line?* More than two lines? Most homes are prewired for two lines. If you require more, the additional lines will have to be installed. The next jump, typically, is to a six-line box.

2. *Is my work space limited?* You may want an integrated answering machine rather than a separate unit.

3. *Will I need to communicate with family members?* Do I have to let them know where I'm going and what needs doing? Will I want to leave messages for myself to jog my

memory? You may want a phone with a personal memo option.

4. *Will I need to share information simultaneously with people at different locations?* You may need conference calling.

5. *If I have two phone lines, do I want a different message left on each?* You may need an answering machine that provides a separate tape for each line.

6. *Should I be able to talk on the phone and have both hands free?* You may want a speaker phone.

7. *Am I going to spend most of my day on the phone?* You may want a headset. When you leave the house, you may need a cellular phone.

8. *Will I have to move around when I'm on the phone?* Will I need to answer the business line(s) quickly regardless of which part of the house I'm in? You may not be able to do without a portable phone.

WHAT ABOUT FAX MACHINES? Ask yourself these questions:

1. *Are all my outgoing faxes going to be generated on a computer?* You may want a computer with an internal fax.

2. *Is working space a limitation?* You may want a small or vertical fax machine.

3. *Will I be sending many multipage documents?* You may need a multisheet feeder to spare yourself the time-con-suming task of feeding documents by hand singly.

4. *Will my faxes be going to phone lines that are often busy?* You may want a machine that automatically redi-als until the line is clear.

5. *Do many of the documents I receive involve legal issues?* You may need a plain-paper system as thermal faxes fade with time.

6. *Is my fax machine also going to function as my copier?* Shop for a plain-paper model. If your copying needs are

high-volume or require special features such as reduction, you may need a fax *and* a copier.

7. *Will my fax share my regular phone line?* You may need automatic switching to transfer incoming calls when the fax machine is in operation.

WHAT SHOULD I ASK MYSELF ABOUT COPIERS? These considerations are important:

1. *Will I be reproducing many multipage documents?* You will need a collator.

2. *Is working space a limiting factor?* You may want a copier with a stationary stop that requires less space to operate.

3. *Do I need to reduce and enlarge documents? And how much control will I require?* Choose between machines with fixed-scale or scalable features.

4. *Will I be reproducing large quantities often?* Make sure you can turn out the volume you need in a reasonable time. The machine you choose should have a high page-per-minute rating.

5. *Is my need for copies infrequent and small? Do I really need a copier?* A copy service near you may well be your best resource, particularly if you have more time than money.

HOW TO ORGANIZE YOUR PROFESSIONAL HOME OFFICE

First, consider that most rooms are rectacular. Even when the floor space is square, the typical placement of windows and doors usually leaves usable space that is rectangular. Most office furniture, therefore, is rectangular.

Next, decide whether you want to a.) maximize floor space or b.) break up the room into work areas.

If you need to maximize floor space, place the furniture against the wall in such a way that the longest edge of the unit follows the longest wall.

If you want to divide the space into distinct units—for example, an office space and a conference area—place a piece of rectangular furniture perpendicular to the longest wall in order to divide the room.

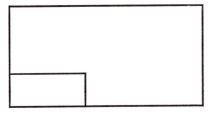

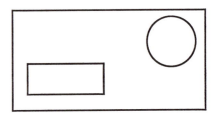

Maximize overall floor space.   Divide room into work areas.

Also, if your intent is to maximize your work space, it's a good idea to place furniture of approximately the same height in an "L" or "U" shape in the room.

Then position equipment on the furniture on a frequency-of-use basis. Obviously, whatever you handle most will be within closest reach. Some filing space—a desk drawer, file crate, or cabinet—should also be readily accessible from the desk.

Create a workspace, then, that says *professional office* to you, one that's mentally, emotionally, and physically pleasing.

Invest in aesthetics and comfort as well as function.

You'll reap dividends in satisfaction and productivity.

CHAPTER TEN

ALL IN THE FAMILY:

WORKING ALONE

TOGETHER

BR-R-R-NG! At last! The call from that purchasing agent Bob Hart's been chasing all year. A regional sales representative, who works from his home, Hart has hovered over the phone all morning like a buzzard circling its next meal. But when the call finally comes, he's halfway across the room. His four-year-old daughter beats him to the receiver. Why, he mutters to himself, do children have the uncanny knack of being by the phone on life-and-death occasions such as this? "Hi, I'm Wendy! My dad's making me a peanut butter and jelly sammitch. Bye!" Slam. Aaarrggh!

BR-R-R-NG! Sally Pierce almost lets the answering machine take the message but changes her mind on the third ring. It might be her client calling back, asking her to include something else with the revised proposal and financial data she has to express-mail to New York this afternoon or six months of work goes down the drain. No problem, Pierce reassures herself as she picks up the receiver. Everything's printed out and she has just enough time to drive the envelope to the FedEx office nearby. But what's that smeared all over the scattered pages of the material she'd stacked so neatly on the dining room table? It looks like Hershey bar drool! And where's little Brian? Aaarrggh!

BR-R-R-NG! The damn phone again! Accountant Ann Rogers grabs it, thinking it's her best client who's been waiting for the earnings report she promised to fax an hour ago. It isn't the client, though, but hubby Ralph, pleading that he's been held up at the office and would she mind picking up the suit and shirts he needs for his early-morning business trip to Denver tomorrow? Trouble is, the cleaner closes in 15 minutes. "Gimme a break!" she screams, slamming down the receiver.

RI-I-I-ING! It's the doorbell. Systems analyst Dan Boyd opens the front door. There's a guy standing there in bib overalls and a cap with RALPH'S PLUMBING on it. "Hi," says the plumber. "Mrs. Boynton said you'd be home and would let me into her house." It will only take a minute and Boyd wonders why he feels such resentment. But he knows it's because his concentration has been broken. He takes the plumber next door, then hurries back to the computer in his attic office. "No-o-o-o-o!" he screams at the blank screen. "I turned it off for you, Daddy," says five-year-old Tammy, beaming up at him.

HANDLING THE HOME/OFFICE CAREER/FAMILY CONFLICT

The possible scenarios are endless, but in this case, the script calls for putting the family in its place. It sounds harsh, downright contradictory to the telecommuter's dream of merging home and office, career and family into a symbiotic blend of harmonious bliss. But without a proper blend—unless each factor fits snugly into the overall equation—the rosy dream can fade to black. It's up to you not to let it happen.

First off, don't kid yourself about the children. No doubt, you love them to pieces. After all, they're one of the primary reasons you're working from home in the first place. But having them underfoot when there's business at hand gets very old very quickly.

WHAT TO DO WHEN THE KIDS ARE AT HOME

The challenge comes in merging incompatible elements. Both your family and your work demand focused, loving attention. Providing it to one or the other is demanding enough. Giving it to both at the same time is well nigh impossible.

Readers of the business section of a New York daily last year encountered several photographs that would have qualified among those once-popular visual puzzles that asked, "What's wrong with this picture?" The photos merged two highly incongruous elements: Working adults and children at play.

One of the pictures depicts a banking executive in her early thirties at a personal computer in her Brooklyn home. Next to her is her four-year-old son, at whom she gazes adoringly. Mother and child are in what appears to be the youngster's playroom, engulfed in a clutter of toys. She's seated rather uncomfortably on a small chair facing a narrow ledge on which are perched her computer and a small lamp, with little room for anything else alongside.

In this improbable setting the newspaper reporter depicts the telecommuter as "one moment handling the accounts of banks in Australia and New Zealand, and at the next moment attending to the needs of her two children."

"At home, I am a mommy and a banker," says the executive. "It is," she adds, "a wearing situation." For sure.

How to Alternate Responsibilities

Further along in the newspaper piece, readers discover how Ms. Banker/Mom copes: Not by combining her two occupations but by judiciously alternating them. She keeps them together by effectively *separating* them, as home workers in the bosom of their families inevitably must.

Paid on the basis of a four-day week, her agreement calls for putting in three full days at a downtown office and two half-days at home. (Arrangements of this sort are increasingly popular. There are now some 6.6 million telecommuters, according to LINK Industries—company employees who work in their homes either part-time or full time.) In the banking executive's case, the two half-days at home consist of the last hour in the morning—usually spent checking with the main office via a computer link and conferring on the phone with business colleagues and clients—followed by three hours of detail work in the early afternoon.

The afternoon slot is critical to her work-from-home success, the executive explains, for it is then that her older son is in nursery school and her toddler usually takes his longest nap. During these periods she can concentrate on her work in blissful solitude.

WHEN YOU NEED IT, ASK FOR HELP. Sometimes the four-year-old will play quietly by himself while she's working, the story notes, but Ms. Banker Mom doesn't count on it because young children aren't considerate in that way. When her workload gets too heavy, she brings in a baby-sitter. Other times she calls on neighbors and friends. When her work spills into the evening, hubby takes care of the children.

Describing her routine as "draining," she justifies it on the basis of minimizing her time away from the children while pursuing a worthwhile career. But the hard reality is that she does her best work when her children aren't around. She telecommutes for *them,* yet they are the primary *obstacles* to her success as a telecommuter. It's a paradoxical fact of life most homeworkers with young children have to resolve.

ESTABLISH A ROUTINE. In *Ms.* magazine, Melissa Fay Greene compares her previous working regimen as a childless author to her current routine as a mother attempting to work at home:

> Before I had children, I spent many hours each day gearing up to write. I read Homer and Chaucer and Browning while the coffee brewed, a stack of notebooks and a set of fine-point pens on the table beside me. At a certain moment, immersed in the poetry, I rose, poured the coffee and warmed my hands around it; took a sip and then, almost trancelike, began to write. I could write until dusk, until midnight.
>
> I don't follow that schedule anymore. Up at 6:45, dress this one, dress that one, lay out clothes for one over there, dash down and back up the basement stairs with fresh socks, feed the cats, let out the dog, braid hair, tie shoes, listen for *honk!* of first car pool, pack lunch, listen for *honk!* of second car pool, load up car to drive third car pool, drive home, sprint into office, gulp coffee, write deathless prose, watch clock, time's up, leave to drive afternoon car pools, and so forth. Occasionally I speed-read a verse of Yeats while making the bed I am about to sit on to write, but there's really no time for anything more.

Working in the embrace of one's family means constantly weighing "More is better!" against "Too much of a good thing."

Don't Become Your Own Worst Enemy

It might be hard but necessary for you to accept that your fervent wish to merge work and family may not be enough to turn desire into reality—and that you as a dynamic business person may be your dream's own worst enemy.

"Just as male boomers are nearing the peaks of their careers," notes Sue Shellenbarger in *The Wall Street Journal*, "many are feeling rising pressure to spend more time with their families. Growth in the number of mothers in the work force is one reason. Rising interest in fathering and a desire to balance work and personal life are also driving the change.

"But as the men strive for balance," she points out, "many are finding that the things they are paid to do well at work create disaster at home. Many find it impossible to prevent workplace problems from spilling over into home life. And the managerial skills they exercise at the office can actually hinder their efforts to draw closer to family members."

What's the answer? There is more than one, but for starters a little empathy can help. Shellenbarger tells of a manager who switched roles with his family members for a while. What he learned from the experience in his own words: "As I watched my 10-year-old daughter portraying me, strutting around, barking orders, demanding that everyone be quiet so I can concentrate, I had to laugh." But when the manager assumed his daughter's role and began feeling resentment, he decided he had to change some of his behavior.

Walking a while in your family's moccasins can take you a long way.

WHAT TO DO WHEN YOU BOTH
WORK AT HOME

When I interviewed Mark Schoening and Laurel Rogers, they were about to undertake two formidable challenges together. Capping an eight-year relationship during which they lived apart, they planned to get married—*and* work from home—side by side, under the same roof.

Rogers, 33, a graphic designer with an electronic publishing firm, would continue to telecommute, dividing the time between her firm and her office in one of the two bedrooms in Schoening's small house. Schoening, who had worked from an office at his home for the past year, would continue to do so in a corner of the dining room.

"I may be seeing this through rose-colored glasses," Schoening said, "but I'm really looking forward to it. I like my life and my work spliced exactly as they are. I'm perfectly content at home. I know I have to work alone to be creative." He enjoys taking an occasional break to mow the lawn or do some other household chore.

He feels no need to get away, he said. "Being home seems the most natural thing in the world to me. With Laurel here, it will be even better."

Accommodating Different Work Styles

Rogers isn't so sure. For one thing, she's usually up early, by 6:00 A.M., even 5:00, and likes to be working soon after. Schoening prefers to wake up "naturally," around 8:00, he said, and start work around 9:00. Trouble is, her office will be right next to their bedroom. "Are you a noisy worker?" he asked his fiancée, cocking his head at her.

Another potential problem is that Schoening's office will be centrally located in the house, on a direct line between the kitchen and the living room. "I head for the fridge when I'm stressed," Rogers said, "so I hope the traffic pattern won't be a problem."

Scoening pointed out that he enjoys listening to classical music, played loudly, while he works, which might preclude someone else trying to concentrate nearby. "But I can stay upstairs until he's done," said Rogers. These are minor considerations easily remedied, the couple agreed. A source of greater conflict could be their individual temperaments.

GETTING IN SYNC. "I like being with other people," she revealed. "I like the synergy, motivation, and energy that comes from working in a group. Things are ideal for me right now. I can go into the office, check with the boss, attend meetings, catch up on what's happening, and feel connected—a real part of the team. That's important to me. On the other hand, the office is crowded and when I'm ready to work, I can head home for four or five hours of pure concentration."

What are the potential problems?

While Rogers is off getting her fill of human contact and stimulation, Mark is home alone, working away contentedly. But when Rogers gets home she'll be ready to hunker down in solitude, while Mark may be looking for some of the conversation and camaraderie she just left behind.

It's no different from one spouse coming home from the office looking for peace and quiet and a bit of space, while the other's "up to here" with it and wants the exact opposite.

The point is that mutual awareness, respect, consideration, willingness to communicate, and compromise are as vital to the success of their working relationship as to their marriage. The two will need to extend their consideration for each other's feelings and needs that much further.

It's what Susan and Jerry Fletcher had to do.

Susan Fletcher, 43, author of *Dragon's Milk* and other children's books, had long been used to having the run of the house. Her husband, a 52-year-old advertising account executive, had gone off to work each morning, and when their daughter, Kelly, left for school, she'd settle comfortably into her writing, kept company only by the family's black cat, Nimbus.

Then Jerry Fletcher traded in his job as a CEO for his 10-second commute, moving his new marketing-advertising consulting business into a spare bedroom of the house. Overnight, his wife was jarred out of her comfortable routine.

"After 16 years of marriage, we thought we knew each other pretty well," he remarks with a chuckle. "We found out just how much we still had to learn after we started working alone together."

They did know each other well, Jerry concedes, but at "home." Now they had to learn to respect each other's needs, desires, and idiosyncrasies at "work." They had to regard one another as if enclosed in plexiglass—visible but apart, present but unapproachable. They had to learn to treat each other's "space" as precious and fragile. Unassailable.

YOUR SPACE OR MINE? His way of concentrating is to pace, to walk around while he problem-solves, Fletcher explains. His wife's method is to sit quietly. "One of the first things we had to learn was that one couldn't stroll up and start a conversation simply because the other wasn't 'doing' anything.

"We had to get absolutely clear in our minds that at certain times of the day and evening, our home is an office in every sense of the word. During those times, the rules of etiquette and behavior are quite different indeed—and have no bearing on our married life."

Fletcher cites an unbreakable rule: "If either of our office doors is closed, the other person doesn't enter—doesn't even knock—honoring it as a sign of total absorption. If either of our doors is open, the other still tiptoes in, aware of possibly intruding on the other's creative thoughts. Whether or not we're actually absorbed doesn't matter. What counts is that one of us has entered the other person's office," he stresses.

Respect and Communication: Two Keys to Success

"If Susan waves me away with a 'Don't bother me, I'm thinking' gesture, I go," adds Fletcher, who is the current president and a founding member of the Association of Home Businesses, an independent, nonprofit organization headquartered in Portland, Oregon. "She does the same for me. No hard feelings. It's a matter of mutual respect that has nothing to do with our personal relationship."

Another hard-and-fast rule is that they fix their own lunches. Neither takes it for granted the other will do it. "We often eat together, and one might invite the other to share a sandwich or salad, but we don't assume anything except that we'll take care of ourselves."

The most important thing is that they have discussed these things and will continue to do so, Fletcher concludes. In fact, they've talked about working alone together with quite a few people. Both have delivered a number of speeches on the subject.

"We've made a real effort to understand where the home ends and the office begins—and *when*," says Fletcher, a member of the

National Speakers Association. "If Susan's manuscript is spread across the dining room table, then it's her work space. If I'm putting together a proposal on the kitchen counter, it's my work space. No questions asked. The other person goes somewhere else."

A real bonus they've accrued from attempting to understand and accommodate each other is that they've strengthened their marriage considerably by learning to communicate more skillfully, Fletcher concludes. They're not alone in this regard.

FAMILY TIME/WORK TIME: SEPARATE IS ESSENTIAL

In an American Home Business Association survey, 97 percent of the respondents indicated that working from home had made the family closer. But they, like the Fletchers, have had to do it by dividing the time they spend at home into separate and distinct compartments, one of them not devoted to the family at all.

Affirms Roxanne Farmanfarmaian, a *Working Woman* contributing editor, "Though you will be physically present more of the time, work will regularly demand your exclusive attention."

This can come as a shock to other members of the family, says Tom Miller, director of the Home Office Research Program at LINK Resources. "Family perceptions of the person working at home go through an evolution," he observes. "In my case, because my family saw so much of me while I was working, the real time I spent with them seemed diminished in value."

His children even asked him once if he could find another job so he'd be able to see them more often.

Entrepreneur Marshall Levin jokes about having to wear a button with "Daddy" on it so his children know what to call him when he finally gets home. No doubt, many executives on corporate fast-tracks feel the same way. The twist here is that Levin works alone and can dictate his own hours. But not really.

Working from home doesn't automatically assure you more time with the family. That's how the dream starts. Sadly, it can end with 9-to-5 becoming 8-to-10, with Saturdays thrown in, maybe Sundays too. Unless you make it a personal priority to schedule adequate family time, your primary reason for working from home becomes the dream's first failure.

There's a silver lining to this problem in that the entire family can learn how to communicate more skillfully and to interact less selfishly. Furthermore, the children are provided with daily role models to help them properly apportion their time for work, play, friends, recreation, and family responsibilities. In this extremely instructive setting, children also learn to be more independent. They can be made to feel they are real and valued contributors to the success of their family unit.

Recognize Potential Conflicts Before They Occur

Another risk, cautions marketing vice president Dean F. Shulman, is that home workers may start to treat spouses and children as employees whose job it is to "perform" for them.

"Foreparents," novelist Don Wallace calls them—homeworkers who harness their families as work units for substantial portions of the day. These tasks, notes Wallace in *Home Office Computing*, aren't legitimate chores and responsibilities, rightfully delegated, but jobs tantamount to putting a child on the treadmill too early in life.

"Kids suffer burnout, too," cautions Wallace.

"Superparents" is the name Wallace gives to home workers who dole out another form of child abuse—plopping their infants and toddlers in playpens or in front of the TV set for hours at a time.

"They want to believe that it is possible to singlehandedly provide preschool children with love, attention, and education while simultaneously running a successful home-based business," says Wallace. "Those in this category are either trapped in a myth or seeking their own ego gratification."

What they do, instead, is deny their children's developmental needs. Wise mothers and fathers respect the maxim, "A child's work is play."

KEEP YOUR GOALS IN MIND. Keep in mind, Dean Shulman advises in *Psychology Today*, that a child creating problems around the house or doing poorly in school isn't a nonperforming subordinate, but your child. Nor is it your family's primary responsibility to make you a more effective manager or entrepreneur. Actually, it's the other way around. One of your main goals as a home worker is probably to become a more caring, more involved parent or spouse.

"Inevitably," predicts Roxanne Farmanfarmaian, "bringing your work into the home *will* create conflicts with the rest of the household. After all, you will be competing, in a sense, for control of an environment previously devoted to domestic pursuits."

Questions that will arise: "Where should the children play? Where must they *not* play? Who can use what phone (or phone line), and at what times? Who does the laundry? Who makes dinner? Who picks up the kids? Who walks the dog?"

For some parents who work from home, the sound of children crying or arguing when they're unable to intervene, or laughing and playing when they can't join in, is disconcerting.

"How do you explain to a two-year-old," asks Tom Forester of Griffith University in Queensland, Australia, "that daddy in the kitchen making a cup of coffee is thinking about his next paragraph and is not to be interrupted?"

When you interrupt your work to socialize with the kids, it's not always easy to go back to your desk and get up to speed again. There can be real difficulty in sustaining an intensity level at home. The knack isn't learned in a day, or even a month. And some people never pick it up. But you have to adjust or you'll fail. Ultimately, you may have to compromise and work alone away from home.

An estimated 20 percent of the people who try telecommuting throw in the towel. Most of them cite the inability to concentrate, particularly in an environment shared by spouses and children.

How to Handle Conflict When It Does Occur

"When you live and work with your family," affirms Frederick H. Rice, director of Kansas State University's Small Business Development Center, "things are bound to get tense." Monitor your family relationships closely, he advises, and make necessary adjustments.

A study of 14,000 women who worked (or wanted to work) from their homes confirms that telecommuting and child care are usually combined with tremendous difficulty. Kathleen Christensen of City University of New York found that half the women who made the move still pay someone to mind the kids.

"By most formal and informal accounts," observes *Esquire* contributing editor Donald R. Katz, "the idea of being a productive worker and a good hands-on mother at the same time is the stuff of myth.

"My friend Eileen tried it, and she ended up attempting to log her eight hours on a computer connected to the corporate miniframe in portions of every hour of the day and night because the baby's naps were short. Eventually she went back to the office part-time, in part because she missed the sounds that adults make."

DECOMPRESS: CREATE GROUND RULES. Along with the usual stresses of working together, couples leashed to each other by a small business have esoteric pressures and demands. Paramount among them is the need to distance themselves from each other, particularly as business partners, both physically and emotionally, regularly and often. Call them periods of decompression.

"There were times during those first two years," wails Dee Sherwood, "when I wanted to leave the business, leave him, leave the *planet!*" The 46-year-old software designer tells how her 17-year marriage to 48-year-old computer programmer Jack Sherwood barely survived their working together. They operated out of a roomy duplex apartment for four years before shifting their successful two-person firm to a downtown office building.

"Part of the problem," explains Dee, "stemmed from the fact that I'm goal-oriented and like to feel forward movement. Jack's more lateral-minded. He's happy exploring, not really concerned about the outcome of a project. I want to *run* our business, to achieve the bright potential I see for it. He wants to *experience* it. Working together almost drove us crazy, not to mention very far apart."

Spouses working together could experience relief about their differences by studying the Hermann Brain Dominance Profiles contained in Laurie Nadel's *Sixth Sense: The Whole-Brain Book of Intuition, Hunches, Gut Feelings and Their Place in Your Every*

Day Life. Reports Nadel: "In a study of more than 500 married couples, Ned Hermann found that in 75 percent of the couples, husband and wife had markedly different brain profiles. In less than 20 percent of the couple profiles were there any significant similarities."

So we *are* different, markedly so. And those who work alone together must keep this fact prominently in mind. "The more aware spouses are of one another's ways of thinking, perceiving, learning and taking action, whether immediately or downstream in life," observes poet Alexandra Kristall, "the easier it becomes for them to appreciate and turn their strengths *and* differences to their mutual advantage."

To survive each other, the Sherwoods wound up creating a few ground rules:

- We will have no business discussions after 6:30 P.M., regardless of whether one or the other is still working on a project. There will be *no* exceptions to this rule.

- We will deliberately and demonstratively show respect for each other's talents, feelings, opinions, and contributions.

- We will make a conscious effort to separate our personal and business relationships. "We began reminding each other, voluntarily and often, that sacrificing our marriage for the business just wasn't worth it," says Jack.

- Each of us will spend a brief period alone at the end of the business day. "It really helps," says Dee. "I may read for a while, play with the cat, go for a short walk, start dinner, whatever, but I don't even *look* at Jack. Not until I'm ready. And when I finally do, I see him as my *husband*, not a business associate, and I behave accordingly."

KNOW WHEN TO STOP. Events planner Colleen Kenmore, 46, a partner with her 48-year-old husband, Gary, in the public relations agency they operate from a suite in a suburban office complex, says they made it "an absolute law" a long time ago to be able to tell each other when and where to get *off* the subject of work. "It's O. K. for either of us to tell the other, 'Hey, it's 7 o'clock—can we let it *go* already?'"

A reassuring touch or hug can take the edge off sounding like a nag, someone who only cares about business as usual. A private, funny saying or gesture, something decidedly friendly, could be a mutual signal for, "That's it, folks! Let's call it a day."

The Kenmores both realized early on it was critical they turn their attention to other things besides work. "We spend so much time together," says Colleen, "that we need to make a constant, conscious effort to talk about other things—family, friends, politics, current events, the weather, whatever. Anything but business at every waking moment!

"Running a small company by yourselves, with so much to do at all times, it's easy to let the work swallow you up. And it will if you don't guard against it. If it happens enough, it can be disastrous."

GET AWAY FROM EACH OTHER. Something else the Kenmores try to do regularly, with each other's blessing, is to get away from each other. Just for awhile. "When you not only live but work together, you can start to feel you're joined at the hip. It's not a pleasant feeling, and you have to deliberately fight it," she says.

They do by having lunch apart, except when business imperatives force them to break the rule. In addition, if one goes to the office on a weekend, the other stays home. They also commute to work separately. When they used to take the same car, Jack relates, Colleen would have the whole day arranged for them while they were still on the freeway. Or they'd immediately pick up a business problem they'd relinquished the night before.

"The drives to and from work got horrible," he says with a grimace. "They were exhausting."

SET REALISTIC EXPECTATIONS. "When the pressure builds— when you've spent a 12-hour day together and it's your fourth such day in a row—it's hard not to build up some resentment," her husband adds. "How do you get rid of it? Most people leave it at the office—at least they do if they're smart.

"But for us, the person at home is the same person at the office, and it's easy to unload the negative feelings on your partner because there's no one else around. If you make a habit of doing that, you're in serious trouble."

"We have a double marriage—personal and business," interjects Colleen Kenmore, "and one of the requisites of a successful marriage is not to have false or unrealistic expectations of your spouse or yourself. The same applies to a business marriage."

She sighs. "We're human beings, not sitcom characters. We have to get past TV's version of 'normal' personal and business relationships. We have to accept that we're not always going to be warm, witty, wise, wonderful, tolerant, incredibly resilient characters.

"We have to have realistic expectations based on real life. We have to acknowledge our shortcomings as well as our talents—the good things and the not-so-good things about ourselves and our partners. It helps prevent business divorce as well as personal divorce," Kenmore concludes.

BEFORE YOU BEGIN, MAKE SURE IT'S WHAT YOU—AND YOUR FAMILY—WANT. Personnel managers agree on one thing about telecommuters: They have to *want* to do it. And that goes double for those trying to do it in the midst of children and spouses. These individuals must be mature, responsible individuals—real performers.

Businesses require exceptional managers as well because their thinking has to change—from keeping direct tabs on their employees to measuring the quality of the work. What's more, to make telecommuting succeed, supervisors have to select jobs that are quantifiable by the results produced.

Managers and telecommuters both agree on the key ingredient of successful telecommuting—faith and confidence in each other. Plenty of it.

"You must have a strong, implicit trust in these employees," remarks Doug Burgum, president of a North Dakota software publishing firm, "and be confident they can have self-discipline at home."

Spouses who work at home together are no less than "remarkable in their belief in themselves, in their families and in their future," says Vian Milehand, a national marketing manager with AT&T who has tracked the home office market since 1981. "They think they can make positive changes in their lives as well as in their communities."

Nonetheless, they still need children who are seen and not heard during business hours; who are fully sensitive to such things as impending deadlines, demanding supervisors, and intolerant clients; who don't have the uncanny knack for being hungry or wanting attention or needing to be chauffeured at the most inopportune times.

Couples working alone together don't need spouses who wish they were somewhere else, who inform them wryly, "I married you for better or worse, but not for lunch;" who used to breathe a sigh of relief when they drove off and now resent them for being around all the time; who berate them for leaving the house in a mess despite the meaningful work they achieve in the process.

The attitude is "Well, you were home all day, you could at least have done a few chores."

And they don't need neighbors and friends who regard them as available at a moment's notice to take over the kids' car pool or come by for a midafternoon chat, as if it were the most natural thing in the world to do.

FIVE ESSENTIALS WHEN YOU WORK ALONE TOGETHER

1. *Demand respect.* Like Rodney Dangerfield, Fran FitzSimon had a tough time earning respect, especially from those closest to her. Money—no problem—the freelance graphic designer makes more of it working from home than she ever did associated with design studios in her native Canada and later in Los Angeles.

But other people's esteem for her home-based activities came much harder.

"The feeling is you don't have a *real* job, so it's O. K. to just drop in," says FitzSimon. "When my husband Ken gets sick or has a day off, he thinks of it as *home*. House guests definitely think of it as home. But for me, weekdays, it's strictly the *office*."

FitzSimon feels she's finally earned the esteem she deserves and, in fact, *needs* to function effectively as a career person working from home. She's achieved her hard-won respect by making it clear to her husband, neighbors, and friends that hers, indeed, is a real job and a real business, deserving of the consideration and courtesies typically accorded business managers and professionals.

Tell your family, neighbors, and friends exactly what you expect from them as a professional operating out of a bona fide business office, which also happens to be a residence. That you'll tolerate nothing less. Tell them it's nothing personal—strictly business, at least during working hours. Go as far as to fly a special flag or windsock from your office window to signal that you're working.

Unfortunately, the education process is never-ending, especially where children are concerned, but it comes with the franchise.

2. *Impose rules.* Lay down the law, firmly but lovingly. Let everyone concerned know what chores you expect done. What rooms are off-bounds and when. What equipment can't be touched, ever. How you want the phone answered, how you expect them to let you know the call is for you. (No hollering!) That good manners and proper decorum are expected whenever company comes, be it grandma or one of mom's clients. Explain why clients are *very* important people.

Remind yourself that mannerly, disciplined children are worth the effort, for their sake as well as yours.

In corporate offices, they're called "job descriptions," presented to new employees, discussed with them in detail and used to grade individual performance during salary reviews. Make up your own job descriptions. Your family members don't work for you, but they're certainly part of the business. And how well they behave during working hours certainly has an impact on your success as a home worker.

3. *Build a strong support system.* Like Tennessee William's Blanche DuBois, you'll be relying on the kindness of others—strangers, family, friends, baby sitters, carpoolers. Make sure you have enough of them on hand, along with adequate backups in times of emergency. Don't figure on Billy or Susie never getting sick or needing an unscheduled lift. Count on it happening at the worst possible times where your business is concerned.

Face it, you're going to be a *needy* neighbor, friend, and spouse, sowing I.O.U.s like a farmer spreading seed in his field. All you can do is be extremely grateful for favors rendered, large and small. And redeem yourself when you can; pay back in kind. Be as accommodating, considerate, and flexible a hubby, neighbor, parent, and friend as you can, because you'll want that kindness, consideration, and flexibility paid back in full. Probably tomorrow morning.

4. *Clean up your act.* "Home Workers Are a Bunch of Slobs." This was the headline of a *Wall Street Journal* story on how a growing number of Americans are working from home offices, and making a total mess of them. "People who work at home occupy

some of the nation's sloppiest and most disorganized offices," claims Sue Shellenbarger.

Bum rap or not, the *WSJ* reporter's subsequent observation certainly rings true: "The disarray can shatter the harmony between work and home life many home-office workers hope to achieve."

In her humorous article, Shellenbarger cites as a case in point Lorice Quong, a farm controller in Eagle, Idaho, who likens her home office to the Boise city dump. Mrs. Quong says her husband's blood pressure used to rise every time he passed her office.

Realize that messiness can be a tremendous stress to other members of your household. It may be your office, and you may be trashing it on behalf of your clients, but no one enjoys living by a landfill or, even worse, stuck in the middle of one.

If your clutter tends to go amok, try to keep the paper monster securely locked in the office. Better yet, clean up your act!

5. *Be tolerant.* Walk a while in your spouse's sandals when he or she gets home from work. You've spent all day in the tranquillity of your office at home, and you're ready for the opposite—some excitement, attention, conversation, stimulation, camaraderie.

Your spouse may have had eight hours of all that, however, and is looking for some of the peace and quiet you've enjoyed all day. Be sensitive to where you both are, physically and emotionally, at the end of the day, and act accordingly.

As a home worker, you may be ready for a party, while she's ready to collapse. Realize that she might consider going out dancing or to dinner or a movie or going out, period, as unreasonable. Try to understand why.

TALKING YOURSELF INTO SUCCESS: SELF-ACTUALIZATION TECHNIQUES

Jack Nicklaus calls it going to the movies in his head, mentally rehearsing critical moves and actions to perfect them. He never makes a golf shot without first hitting the ball in his mind. He sees himself swinging the club. He watches the ball arc high in the air. He sees it land and roll across the green, gentling to a stop by the pin, so close to the hole it's almost a tap-in. Only then does he go through the motions himself.

San Francisco surgeon Ira Sharlip also runs motion pictures of the mind. He does it the day before he performs a difficult operation. "I visualize it step-by-step from initial incision to final suturing," he says.

Gerald Epstein, a physician who treats physical and emotional problems with visual imagery, claims the brain doesn't know the difference between an actual and imagined event.

Rehearsing over and over in your head what you'd like to accomplish in real life does work, assures Shakti Gawain, who writes and lectures on using mental affirmation to effect positive changes in the fields of health, education, business, athletics, and the creative arts.

Make It Happen:
Rehearse Your Success

Conjure up your own image of success, Gawain urges in her book, *Creative Visualization*. Focus on the idea or picture regularly, "giving it positive energy until it becomes objective reality—until you achieve what you have been visualizing."

Visualization is simply the creation of a picture in your mind of a successful outcome, says Steven Ungerleider, co-author of *Beyond Strength*, a guide for coaches and motivational experts on the growing importance of psychological training in competitive sports. And by creating the image often enough, we make it happen.

It's a process akin to the technology of the home-video player, Ungerleider points out in *Psychology Today*: "Your brain acts as its own unique VCR, scanning your memory for images, using all the sensory input to collect and shuttle them onto the screen of your imagination.

"Unlike a VCR, however, our internal equipment, when trained and used properly, will recall visual, auditory, kinesthetic, and an assortment of other input with ease. These images form a 'mental blueprint' for the event and later interact with new images in order to shape goals for improved performance."

How to Create a Mood for Success

Our moods can be easily triggered by the images and events we all carry in our subconscious, claims Oakland, California sales trainer Susan E. Dailey. And we can shape those images to put ourselves in the best mood for success. The goal, says Dailey, is to achieve peak performance by dealing with our unconscious doubts and fears.

"Have you ever noticed that star athletes often stop and close their eyes and become very still right before they start?" asks San Francisco consultant Arthur S. Giser. They're practicing guided imagery.

Karl Malone not only closes his eyes, he talks to himself each time he steps up to the free-throw line. If you've watched the NBA star on TV, you've seen him move his lips just before he lofts the ball to the basket. No one knows for sure what he's saying or why, but it's safe to assume he puts himself through a form of mental calisthenics before attempting each free throw.

Talking to himself obviously works. The words Malone mouths silently must help him concentrate and replicate his fluid motions flawlessly, for the Utah forward's free-throw conversions are consistently among the highest in the league.

Mental Drills Plus Practice Equal Success

Patricia Megan Pingree, a licensed professional counselor in Portland, Oregon, cites a study involving, appropriately enough, free throw shooters. She tells of four groups of basketball players formed to test the growingly popular hypothesis that creating mental pictures of a desired outcome can, indeed, positively affect that outcome.

The four groups were measured in their free-throw proficiency. Then, one group of shooters engaged in mental drills of shooting free throws along with physically practicing the shots. The second group visualized making free throws but didn't actually shoot any. The third group practiced shooting but didn't indulge in visual imagery. The fourth group did not practice, physically or mentally. Eventually the four groups were tested again.

The first three groups improved in their free-throw proficiency, says Pingree, a Smith College graduate with a master's in counseling psychology and a certificate in interactive guided imagery. Predictably, the fourth group didn't improve. The group that physically and mentally rehearsed shooting improved the most. The group that visualized shooting but didn't physically practice improved as much as the group that practiced but didn't do the imagery, she relates.

In *Skiing* magazine, World Cup champion Billy Kidd tells how when he was a high school student in Stowe, Vermont, he would sit for hours visualizing himself on a race course. Whenever he did this, he reports, his performance invariably improved the next time he got on skis. Today, Kidd uses similar mental drills in his racing camps for skiers.

How to Talk Yourself into Success

First, he shows his students videos of championship skiers to give them mental images to copy. Then he instructs the students to put themselves in the racers' boots: "Visualize yourself making round, smooth turns. Look down and check out your body position. Are your knees bent, your feet apart, your hands in front? Now explode out of the starting gate. Feel the snow under your skis. Feel the wind in your face. Feel the centrifugal force on your outside ski. Listen to the sounds coming from your edges."

The technique has produced "phenomenal improvement," says Kidd.

"We talk to ourselves all the time," reminds guided imagery expert Pingree. "Trouble is, we don't engage in pep talks but the opposite. Our inner voice is usually critical and fault-finding. Instead of being nurturing, we beat ourselves up, mentally and emotionally. It's the result of a lifetime of negative conditioning."

Many people set themselves up for failure instead of success, says Pingree, by repeating over and over, 'I can't do this!' 'I'm not smart enough!' 'I don't deserve to win!' 'Who am I kidding?' 'I'll make a fool of myself!' They get so good at convincing themselves they can't win that they actually become proficient at losing. They paralyze themselves with immobilizing self-talk.

"Turn it around," exhorts Pingree.

"Since you're going to talk to yourself, learn to do it in a positive, constructive manner. Put your energy and emotion into visualizing victory instead of defeat. By getting in touch with the wise, compassionate part of ourselves that accepts all our faults and flaws as well as our strengths and skills, we allow our intuitive selves to help us find our answers and solutions."

Pingree puts it another way: "In effect, we're taking the microphone away from our inner critic and turning it over to our inner booster, whose job it is to provide the motivation and support we need to achieve our full potential."

Consult Your Inner Self

As important as learning to talk to ourselves in a positive manner is learning to *listen*, says Pingree.

"Each inner conversation should be a conscious, deliberate two-way communication. To achieve this, you should make regular appointments with yourself. Consider these 'consultations' with your inner self as important as any strategic or planning sessions you might schedule with a marketing consultant, your accountant, or a client."

Take the talks seriously, Pingree urges. "Treat them with the same courtesy and respect you'd accord any other business consultation. Prepare for each session. Select a topic and an agenda. Know, going in, what you want the meeting to cover. Clear away a suitable period of time. Fifteen to 20 minutes a day is all you need. Free yourself of all interruptions. Pick a place in which you feel safe and completely at ease."

Relax Your Way to Success

Finally, use a relaxation process to get yourself in the proper mood, to move your focus from the outer world inward, to a quiet, secure place where you can concentrate fully, Pingree advises. The key to effective imagery, confirms Colorado State University psychologist Richard Suinn, is the deep relaxation that precedes it.

"The more you slow your brain waves," claims Adelaide Bry, author of *Visualization*, "the more relaxed you become, the more you can tune in to your own higher intelligence." She compares it to the dimming of lights in a movie theater, which allows you to see the images on the screen as distinctly as possible. Don't get so relaxed, however, that you fall asleep. Or so focused that you become rigid. Bry describes the desired state as "receptive stillness." Or "relaxed attention."

Guided imagery is as old as human communication itself, says Pingree: "When the shaman drew pictures of hunted animals on the cave walls, when the medicine woman took her patient on an imaginary journey to healing waters, when early agriculturists fashioned fertility icons to ensure an abundant harvest, they were practicing guided imagery."

She describes the process as a mental representation of reality, encompassing as many as five modes of perception—sight, sound, touch, taste, and smell.

"When we worry, fantasize, dream or idealize, we are involved in imagery," says Pingree. "Why not, then, harness its capacity to assist in our problem solving? Why not let it serve our search for insight, our quest for meaning? By using a relaxation process to quiet our habitual circular thinking, we can invite our intuitive intelligence to spawn images pertaining to a chosen topic. We can then engage in interactive communication with those images to achieve the answers we seek."

ON YOUR OWN WITH GUIDED IMAGERY

People who work alone are ideally suited to employ this technique effectively. The reason is that many of the qualities home workers possess are the same factors that facilitate imagery—strong motivation, high expectations of success, self-confidence, emotional openness, and a willingness to try. Home workers usually also have access to a comfortable, relaxing environment, which is essential to the successful performance of the mental exercises.

"By forming an image," explains Stephanie Matthews-Simonton, author of *Getting Well Again*, "a person makes a clear mental statement of what he or she wants to happen. And by repeating the statement, he or she soon comes to expect that the desired event will indeed occur. As a result of this positive expectation, the person begins to act in ways consistent with achieving the desired result and, in reality, helps to bring it about."

Guided imagery exercises can be done simply by reading the script a time or two in order to memorize the gist of it, and then doing the exercise from memory. You can always jog your memory by looking at the script along the way. Obviously, however, the exercises work better when you can *listen* to the script, giving your full attention to your mental, physical, and emotional sensations as they arise in response to what you are hearing.

So have someone read the directions to you. Or you may want to record or have someone else record one or more of the scripts in this book. Or order a professionally recorded version of any or all of the exercises. A recorded version allows you to proceed at your own pace, hitting the "pause" button whenever you want more time to explore the developing story line in your head.

You may find, too, that one introduction works better for you than others. If so, adapt the one you like to the other scripts. Alter and custom-tailor each inner dialogue to suit your own preferences and needs. These scripts are merely an aid to get you started.

Learning to Relax

Don't worry about your capacity to become completely relaxed, advises Pingree. It may take awhile to get the hang of it. Keep trying, though, as the effort will be well worth your new-found ability to unwind at will. Think of the enormous therapeutic benefits to your blood pressure!

Also, how *much* you are able to relax will vary from day to day. Again, the more often you do it, the easier it will become.

Closing your eyes usually helps. The idea is to remove yourself from whatever's "out there" in order to focus on what's "in here." But if closing your eyes makes you uncomfortable, then let your gaze go into "soft focus"—a sort of unfocused stare.

You'll also encounter the term "Signal Breath" in these and other guided imagery scripts. A signal breath is exactly that, a cue you learn to respond to instantly—a signal that moves you quickly and effortlessly into imagery readiness.

It announces to your whole being, "Hey, I'm getting started now! I intend to look and listen *inside* of me." In turn, your mind and body reply, "O. K., we remember how to do this. We're ready to go."

The signal breath starts with a strong, audible exhalation. Push all the air out of your lungs. Then inhale fully, pulling the air into the deepest recesses of your body. Now exhale strongly again. And resume your normal breathing (or whatever meditative breathing rhythm you like).

Painting the Pictures

Once you're relaxed and tuned in to yourself, don't be discouraged if you don't see "pictures" in your mind immediately. It doesn't matter, assures Pingree. "Imagery doesn't have to be visual. Work with whatever does come—a word or a phrase. Or a memory. Or a feeling. Or a 'sense' you can't really describe. Welcome whatever shows up and go with it."

When the visual images do start to occur, practice working with them, she urges. It's a skill, like any other, that can be strengthened through repetition. It may help you to make simple sketches of the pictures in your mind. They don't have to be artistic or even accurate, but creating physical representations of what you see in your head serves several purposes.

The drawings provide a record of images you'll want to review again and again. They provide external support for the internal changes that are occurring. They enhance the learning process by engaging your muscles and involving your aesthetic senses in the mental pictures. They often serve to trigger heightened awareness; for example, you may not realize how powerful you actually are in the face of your obstacles until you see in the picture you've drawn how much larger you are than whatever stands in your way. On the other hand, the sketches can help contain any images that may feel overwhelming.

Consulting Your Advisor

Another term with which you'll become familiar is "Inner Advisor" or "Inner Guide." Freud was the first to refer to it as the *unconscious*—the center of one's psyche, which emotionally directs, regulates, and influences the course of an individual's life. Jung calls it the *self*. In guided imagery, meeting and conferring with your inner advisor means you're in conscious contact with these important mental and emotional resources to which we can all too easily become oblivious. Simply reestablish your ties through imagery.

"For many people," says Matthews-Simonton, "the Inner Guide takes the form of a respected authority figure—a wise old man or woman, a director, a religious figure—with whom they are able to carry on an internal conversation, asking questions and hearing answers that seem to be wise beyond the individual's conscious capacities."

Make your inner advisor Abraham Lincoln, if you like. Or Mahatma Ghandi or Mother Teresa or Yoda or a kindly grandmother you revered as a child. Your inner guide needn't even be human, says Pingree. "It could be an angel or a tree or a chipmunk or the color purple. It's only essential that this imagined resource figure embody at least three crucial characteristics—*compassion, wisdom,* and a *willingness to communicate.*"

Encountering Emotion

Doing guided imagery, especially at first, may trigger an impulse to cry, cautions Pingree: "Sometimes people discover when they relax, let down their guard, and tune in to themselves, that there's *emotion* in there. They've been stuffing it for so long, tending to business as usual, and simply surviving, that when they finally allow themselves the luxury of consulting with themselves about how *they* feel, a sense of tremendous gratitude wells to the surface."

You may want to pause and allow time for the tears and emotion to be released, suggests Pingree. Or you may decide to keep moving forward and return later to the surprisingly deep feelings you've uncovered.

"Just make sure you do return to them," she stresses. Those feelings are important."

USING IMAGERY TO ACHIEVE PERFORMANCE

Charles Garfield, best-selling author and holder of three graduate degrees including a Ph.D. in clinical psychology, also subscribes to intense mental rehearsal as a prelude to success.

"Most people use words to describe their plans and activities, even to themselves," he points out in his best-selling book, *Peak Performers*. "But even more than words, images motivate people to perform at peak efficiency," Garfield writes, citing Albert Einstein as someone who used imagery in his problem solving. The world is familiar with Einstein's famous visualization of a boy riding a beam of light, the image that foreshadowed his Theory of Relativity breakthrough.

Notes Garfield: "Peak performers, particularly in business, sports, and the arts, report a highly developed ability to imprint images of successful actions in the mind. They practice, mentally, specific skills and behaviors leading to those outcomes and achievements which they ultimately gain."

Firewalking on Cool Thoughts

The power of the totally absorbed mind is no less than awesome. The average person can walk through fire unsinged simply by thinking cool thoughts, attests psychologist Ronald J. Pekala, executive director of Pennsylvania's Mid-Atlantic Education Institute.

Pekala led a group of 71 firewalkers over a 12-foot-long, 4-foot-wide pit of fire after giving them six hours of intensive training, primarily in focusing on a single comforting image. Then, one by one, eyes closed, breathing deeply, they treaded mentally on a carpet of dewy moss—and crossed the blazing coals unscathed.

Like guided imagery, the ancient ceremonial custom of firewalking is growing in appeal to motivational trainers around the world, who see it as an excellent way to help people conquer their fears. If you can talk yourself into walking through fire, the thinking goes, you should be able to convince yourself you can do anything else.

When you get this visualization schtick down pat, decide for yourself whether you'd like to tiptoe through a bed of hot coals. I may not join you. But next to firewalking, talking yourself into no longer procrastinating or never again feeling lonely or being highly creative, supremely confident, or eminently successful in your field should be a stroll in the park.

And it's O. K. if you decide guided imagery isn't your cup of tea. Like scotch and oysters, it's a developed taste and not for everyone. What's important, however, is that we learn to talk to ourselves appropriately. And to listen attentively.

If you don't develop a taste for guided imagery, settle for the habit of supporting yourself through private pep talks and other motivational conversations. It's vital for us who work alone. We need to reinforce our convictions and our progress with constant recognition and praise.

"So anoint your new workspace," urges Pingree. "Frame that first check or acceptance letter. Hang a talisman from your desk lamp. Plan a victory party. And invite all your inner advisors to thank them for their continued assistance."

SCRIPTING YOUR SUCCESS

Psychotherapist Pingree has prepared a number of guided imagery "scripts" to help you find your way to where you want to go, personally and professionally—and away from where you don't want to be. Each exercise takes you, step-by-step, through a specific beginning, middle, and ending. Simply follow her instructions on how to breathe properly, relax thoroughly, concentrate deeply, and invite the formation of images that will lead you to the answers you seek.

Script #1: Visualizing Your Success

Begin by setting aside 20 or so uninterruptible minutes. Turn off the ringer on the phone. Make yourself comfortable. Loosen your clothing and settle in to explore and energize yourself in your home office today.

Take a Signal Breath. Start by exhaling forcibly . . . then inhale strongly . . . then exhale again . . . send the message to your body and your unconscious that you're open to learning more about how to succeed on your own.

Let your attention focus gently now on your breathing . . . notice the rhythmic ebb and flow . . . know there is nothing you need to change in this time and place in any way . . . know there is no need to force anything . . . no need to try . . . simply soften and release . . . let your breath flow in and out . . . notice how your thoughts ebb and flow as they enter your conscious mind . . . know that your unconscious mind continues to function even as your conscious mind is aware of the thoughts.

Allow your rhythmic breath to be drawn into your head, filling it with openness and space . . . let go of any tension there might have been in your scalp . . . relax around your eyes . . . around your ears . . . through your jaw . . . feel the softness and warmth flow down your neck . . . across your shoulders . . . into your upper arms . . . draw comfort and ease into your elbows . . . forearms . . . wrists . . . release all discomfort and stress in your body . . . feel it flow out through your hands . . . and fingers . . . and palms . . . let it all go.

Welcome now, as you inhale, the nurturing oxygen into your lungs . . . your heart . . . your solar plexus . . . sense the comfort flowing into the innermost parts of your body . . . fill them with nourishing, healing energy . . . feel that energy curl through your knees and into your calf muscles . . . into your ankles and the soles of your feet, into your toes . . . let each cycle of breath vitalize and cleanse every single cell in your body . . . penetrate the marrow of your bones . . . and radiate out through the pores of your body . . . allowing yourself all the time you need . . . to arrive at just the right level of peacefulness . . . and relaxation . . . for you . . . for today . . . in this time and place.

When you are ready, allow the wisdom of your unconscious mind to offer you an image of your success . . . an image of you working happily, productively and, contentedly in your home office . . . the way you've always dreamed it would be.

Simply extending the invitation for your image to come . . . and then wait, with open expectation, for it to appear . . . as you know the sun rises every day, whether you wait for it or not.

As the image takes form, observe it closely. It may not be what you expected . . . not even be related in any obvious way to your working from home. Enjoy any surprise you might experience and greet what appears with curiosity and a willingness to explore . . . notice the colors, textures, and shapes that make up your image . . . watching for any movement . . . listen for any sounds, noting smells . . . wondering how it would feel to touch the images . . . take all the time you would like to explore the image from all angles . . . in any ways you choose.

Greet your image now . . . communicate with it in whatever way feels right to you . . . let it know you would like to converse about succeeding on your own . . . ask the questions you would like answered: *How do I accomplish this certain thing I very much want? What must I pay more attention to? Less attention to? What am I doing right, and how can I do more? What am I doing that is not effective? What else do I need to know about working alone?*

Allowing your conversation to evolve naturally, effortlessly, in whatever way enhances your sense of what your success is all about.

If it feels comfortable to you, now allow yourself to move inside the image . . . becoming the image . . . experiencing how it feels to *be* your success . . . looking out from inside the experience of succeeding . . . knowing now what it's like . . . feeling in your body and mind how it is to be a success . . . take all the time you want to savor the sensations . . . the feelings . . . the insights . . . then gradually move out of the image . . . bring with you whatever you want to preserve from the experience . . . now close with the image for today in whatever way feels good to you . . . know that you will remember all you need to remember about what has happened today . . . trust that your body and mind will retain the image of your succeeding even when you're not consciously aware of it . . . that your body and mind will help you move toward your goals without your conscious effort or help.

Gently, in the next few minutes, bring yourself back into this room . . . back to this time and place . . . feeling refreshed . . . notice your rhythmic breathing . . . effortlessly draw energy and clarity of purpose into your entire being . . . feel your arms and legs tingling comfortably . . . eager now to rise . . . stretch . . . move toward success.

Alicia Thornton is a 52-year-old fabric artist with a highly successful business. She makes exquisite eyeglass cases, selling her creations, each one unique, to upscale department stores and boutiques where they are scooped up faster than she can replace them. But it wasn't always so.

A year ago, all Thornton had was her creative gift, years of eperience sewing for her family of four, and the wish to earn money using her talents. What she lacked was a clear picture of her goal, the vision to pull herself forward—specifics to turn fantasy into reality.

Guided imagery changed all that for her. Visualizing her success, Thornton saw herself working happily in her sewing room. In the image she summoned for herself, the workspace in her daylight basement was transformed into a much more appealing and efficient setting. Overhead halogen lighting now enhanced the natural light from the windows for true color perception. There was a wide cutting table. And generous shelving with large cubbyholes for storing fabrics. Smaller nooks held beads and an assortment of bright thread. Her sewing machine was positioned perfectly.

For the business side of her operation, there was a comfortable desk and office phone. Her personal computer had been moved, along with a chair, into the basement's spacious, previously unused closet, which now had built-in shelving for her office supplies. Soothing music wafted from a portable CD player.

"How do I accomplish this success?" Thornton asked her successful self, working away serenely in her wonderful new office.

"Isn't it all clear to you?" came the reply. "Just do it!"

"What things do I have to pay more attention to?" Thornton asked.

"Your heart," she heard back.

"What should I pay less attention to?"

"You know the answer to that one too. Disregard your skeptical relatives. Ignore any criticism that isn't constructive. Focus on what *you* want."

"What am I doing that's right?" Thornton asked. "What more can I do?"

"You're doing fine," assured Successful Alicia in Thornton's image. "Continue with your brainstorming group. Follow through on that women's business mentor program you heard about. Get a good portfolio of samples made up. Check in with me often."

"What am I doing wrong?" Thornton persisted.

"Not much, sweetie," came the reply. "Just don't let yourself buy into other people's agendas."

"What else do I need to know about succeeding on my own?"

The answer came as a surprise to Thornton, but in it she heard the ring of truth. "When you really get rolling," said Successful Alicia, "you're not going to want to do all the work yourself. Hire someone to do the scut work, the cutting and sewing, and put your energy into the parts you like best—making decisions about colors and textures, choosing fabrics, and designing all the beadwork and embroidery. But you'll still need to do all the marketing of your products, at least for now."

Most of this information confirmed and supported what Thornton already knew. Some, surprisingly, was brand new to her. But now her vision of success was clear and complete. She saw everything she had to do to achieve it. And she got started.

Script #2: Defeating Procrastination

Begin by making yourself comfortable. Disconnect the phone. Adjust your clothing. Settle into a position that promotes alert relaxation in you.

Take a Signal Breath. Exhale strongly. Inhale deeply. Exhale again. Repeat the sequence if it feels good to you . . . then allow your breathing to fall into whatever rhythm it wants to take . . . know there's nothing you need to do to change it in any way. Now, notice your breath . . . observe it casually, without judgment . . . feel the air as it moves through your nostrils, into the back of your throat, down your windpipe, and into your lungs . . . and back out again.

Be aware of how your chest expands as you inhale, not only to the front, but also high under the breastbone . . . into your back . . . out to each side . . . and deep into your solar plexus.

Feel your whole upper body contract as you exhale . . . feel the rhythmic flow of your breathing . . . allow it to be shallow or deep . . . let it be whatever it wants to be . . . just trust that your body knows how to take care of your needs without your ever having to make it happen . . . allow each cycle of breath to release you into peaceful comfort . . . let the feelings of comfort grow . . . each time you exhale . . . settle closer to the level of relaxation that's just right . . . for you . . . today . . . take all the time you want.

Now, as you're ready, invite an image to form in your mind . . . an image for the part of you that knows all about procrastination . . . an image (let it be a human or an animal, or an object, whatever works and is willing to talk with you about how you procrastinate) . . . and why . . . an advisor that wants to help you understand how procrastination fits into your life.

Let go of any attempt to control the form that this Inner Advisor takes . . . just let it be whatever it is . . . ask for that part of you to step forward, and as it does, express your appreciation for its willingness to confer with you . . . making yourselves comfortable in whatever ways feel right to you and your advisor.

Begin by telling this image what aspect of your procrastination you want to learn about today. Explain what form of avoidance your procrastination takes . . . describe the work you ought to be doing . . . and describe what you do instead of the work.

Now enter a dialogue with your advisor, asking for specific information: *How does this procrastination hurt me? . . . What does it cost me when I perpetually delay? . . . What does it cost me personally? . . . Professionally? . . . Financially? . . . What does my procrastination do to my confidence and self-esteem?*

Allow your advisor to communicate responses to you in whatever ways it chooses.

Let it converse with you, perhaps nonverbally, about the harmful consequences of your procrastination . . . the ways it hurts you . . . take all the time you need to explore the problems you cause yourself by procrastinating.

Then ask yourself how you might *benefit* from your procrastination: *Are there any hidden payoffs? What do I want that procrastinating gets me? What do I get that I like? Does my procrastinating save me from feeling something I don't want to feel? Will I find out something about myself I'd rather not know? What benefit or advantage does my procrastination gain for me in my relationships with others?*

Listen closely now . . . hear what your Inner Advisor tells you about all the things you want to know about your procrastination . . . ask for clarification if you're confused or uncertain about what you hear and feel.

Continue questioning your advisor until you've learned as much as you want to learn today about the possible pay-offs of procrastination.

Now that you've talked over the *costs*, on one hand, and the *benefits*, on the other, of your procrastination, it's time to consider with your advisor whether you *want* to give up procrastinating. Ask yourself: *Is overcoming my procrastination something I just THINK I need to do? Or is procrastinating something I really HAVE to do, whether or not I want to do it? . . . Does procrastinating actually hurt me that much? Can I still achieve my goals, even though it takes me longer when I procrastinate? . . . Or am I just kidding myself about succeeding unless I quit procrastinating? . . . In other words, when I really think about it, am I hurting myself that much when I procrastinate?*

If you and your advisor decide that the manner and severity of your procrastination doesn't warrant further effort, attention, or concern right now, thank your Inner Advisor for helping you.

Agree to confer on the matter again, if it seems necessary, some time in the future.

If you decide you need to proceed with banishing procrastination from your life, confer with your advisor on a few more points. Negotiate, if necessary. For example: *I know the reason I often procrastinate is because the only time I let myself relax is when I'm procrastinating. If you'll help me not to procrastinate, I'll schedule some relaxation time before or after I need to get my work done.*

Continue to negotiate your terms with the advisor until you feel you'll be able to retain some of the benefits you used to obtain through procrastinating . . . only now you'll secure them in more productive ways. If you reach an impasse in your negotiations, try calling in other advisors to help you resolve the remaining problems.

If you feel you need to take a break, agree to meet later for future discussions. Bring this session to a close for now in whatever way feels right to you . . . . acknowledge the progress you feel you've made toward solving your procrastination problem . . . express your gratitude to your advisor for meeting with you today . . . then return gently . . . feeling calm and relaxed . . . to this time and place.

As someone who loves to work alone, preferably outdoors, Arthur Vozinsky has created the perfect job for himself. He works from his home as a residential landscaper-gardener. Earning his living with his hands, doing the kind of physical labor he finds tremendously rewarding, with tangible and beautiful results, procrastination was the least of Vozinsky's problems when he was outside with his tools.

It was inside that he got into trouble. He hated to do his billing. Customarily, Vozinsky receives a 35 percent down-payment on his work when he takes on a project, then bills for the remainder of his fee when the job is done. The trouble was, he hated taking care of this part of his business, often letting so much time elapse before sending out his invoices that customers wound up taking as long to pay him as he did asking them for the money.

Nor did he really blame them. They're like most people, he told himself—they just needed to be reminded. It was his problem, he correctly assessed. But he hated "pestering" others for money.

He hated sitting down and getting the bills out. He'd do almost anything to avoid the task—work in his own garden, fix his son's swing set, empty the dishwasher, fold laundry—anything but the billing.

When he finally asked for an Inner Advisor to help him with his problem, a huge, all-too-familiar slug slimed into view. It proceeded to lambaste him on what his procrastination was costing him, not just financially but in terms of emotional turmoil and his wife's mounting irritation at what she termed "childish" and "senseless" malingering. No denying it. Not bringing in the money he earned was also irrational, demoralizing, and depressing.

When asked what possible benefit there was to his behavior, the huge slug pointed out wisely: "You're like everyone else. You just want to do the fun stuff. When your wife pushes, you respond just like me. You curl up in a tight little ball and refuse to budge. It's your protective mechanism. The more Brenda prods you to do the billing, the more you resist. But you know you've got to start getting your bills out regularly and on time."

Vozinski agreed with the slug. He told Brenda he realized part of his difficulty with billing was his knee-jerk reaction against her attempts to encourage him. He told her he'd ease the chore by tackling it on alternate Tuesday evenings, in front of the TV set, during his favorite mindless shows. He asked for her help in protecting him from other distractions during that time. And he promised her (and the slug) that if this plan proved ineffective, he'd hire someone to spend a couple of hours each month to get the billing done for him. Happily, though, the first plan worked. His relationship with his wife, his self-esteem, and his income improved tremendously.

Script #3: Befriending Solitude

Begin by making yourself comfortable. Withdraw your attention gently from the world outside you. Take a Signal Breath. Exhale strongly, emptying the deepest part of your lungs. Then inhale deeply and exhale strongly again. Do the breath again if it feels good . . . send your mind and body the message that you are opening your receptivity to intuitive ways of knowing and experiencing.

Even as you let your awareness focus on the natural rhythm of your breathing, allow any thoughts that come to mind to enter and pass on through. There's nothing you need to force . . . nothing you have to try to accomplish . . . only soften yourself . . . release any tension . . . let your body and mind simply be, moment to moment.

Imagine a ball of nurturing light that rolls with the cyclical waves of your breath . . . start at your solar plexus and move gently up the front of your body to your head as you inhale . . . then down the back of your body as you exhale . . . each breath bringing an increasing sense of comfort, ease, and relaxation . . . allow the flow of warm light to soothe and soften your mind and body . . . soothe the muscles of your chest . . . your face and scalp . . . your neck and shoulders . . . your rib cage and lower back and pelvis . . . down the backs of your legs and into your feet . . . then up your shins and thighs . . . into your abdomen and belly . . . allow the light to linger at any spot that needs extra loving care.

With each breath, you become more serene, more open.

Give yourself all the time you want to reach the level of comfort that is just right . . . for you . . . for today.

When you're ready, go to a place in your mind. It can be a place you've actually been or one that exists only in your imagination. You're alone there. Let this place be whatever it is . . . a beautiful and happy place, where you enjoy the solitude . . . or a sad and lonely place, where you're not entirely comfortable, but to which you feel drawn today.

Take some time now to explore this place you have chosen . . . experience it fully . . . notice what is there . . . the colors and textures . . . the smells . . . the sounds . . . the movements . . . noticing what the weather is like . . . what time of day it seems to be . . . what you notice about the air on your skin.

Observe casually how your body feels in this place. What's your breathing like? How's your energy level? Your posture? Are your muscles tense or relaxed? Know there is nothing you have to change . . . nothing you need to do . . . know at the same time that you *can* change anything you want . . . if you *want* to . . . make this an experience that's comfortable for you today.

When you're ready, invite someone or something to join you in this place . . . a presence that knows all about your experience of aloneness. Let this being take whatever form it likes, a human, an animal or a thing . . . not caring what shape it takes, so long as this Inner Advisor is all-knowing and compassionate about your aloneness . . . and willing to help you understand and accept *your* aloneness because of what working alone and being on your own mean to you.

As this form appears, greet it in whatever way feels right to you. Explain that you are eager to understand more about working and being alone. Settle in with your advisor, ask about whatever you want to know, and allow time for this being to respond in a way you can understand.

You may want to ask your advisor: *What kind of balance between time spent alone and time spent with people do I need in my life? How much of each is best for me? . . . What kind of contact with others particularly nourishes me? . . . Which activities allow me best to be alone? Problem solving? Physical exercise? Reading? Listening to music? Are there specific people it's important for me to stay connected with? . . . Are there any people whom I should avoid because they add to my loneliness? What do I like best about being alone? . . . How long can I be alone before I usually start feeling lonely? . . . Exactly what is it that makes me feel lonely?*

Listen now for the answers.

Then ask yourself: Are there any other questions I want to address with this Inner Advisor today? Is there anything else my advisor wants to know from me before I close?

If not, finish with your advisor in whatever way feels right . . . come back gradually to this time and place . . . bring with you all the information that's important . . . and feel relaxed . . . alert . . . grateful . . . energized.

Joanne Crain is a sociable, outgoing 34-year-old department manager for a national manufacturer of telephone equipment. As a telecommuter, she is working alone for the first time in her life and sorely misses the social and professional contact she used to enjoy with her office mates.

Often when Crain tries to settle into a stint of productive solitude in the high-tech office of her suburban home, she experiences a rising anxiety, a vaguely uncomfortable feeling that something is missing, that she wants other people near her, not necessarily to talk with, just to be there. In the past, this bright, dynamic executive has held onto negative work and personal relationships out of a sense that any involvement, any contact, was better than none. Now Crain knew in order to succeed at this job, she would have to learn to function contentedly and effectively alone.

When she invited an Inner Advisor on Loneliness to assist her in guided imagery, Sara, her younger sister appeared. After a warm, enthusiastic greeting, Crain asked her first question: "Why do I feel so lonely when I'm alone?"

"Joanne," replied her sibling and new Inner Advisor, "I was born when you were just a year and a half old. We've been inseparable as long as you can remember. I followed you everywhere. We did everything together—remember? There were no other kids around, and mom and dad were always fighting. The two of us created our own little world. We kept each other feeling safe. No wonder you feel as though something is missing when you're alone. You've spent your whole life trying not to feel that way."

From this insightful starting point, Crain went on to explore the full range of her problem with Advisor Sara. As a result, she stopped criticizing herself for feeling lonely. She put a reassuring picture of Sara on her desk to affirm her beloved sister's continuing presence in her life. She scheduled regular times to exercise and to connect often with friends through meetings and by phone. She became more discerning in how she spent her leisure time so that her contacts and activities brought her real support, not merely distractions.

And she learned to savor working alone, reminding herself constantly of all the things she likes best about her solitary lifestyle—the flexible scheduling, the freedom from constant supervision, the luxury of choosing her own pace, the escape from trivial interruptions.

One day, she put her feet up and made a checklist of all the things she treasures about working from home. To her surprise and delight, the list ran a page long. Now whenever she feels the stirrings of loneliness, Crain takes out her list, reads it over, and then goes happily back to work.

Script #4: Building Self-Confidence

In the course of working alone, situations are bound to arise for which we feel ill-prepared or inadequate, yet which are critical to our personal or business progress. The following script is designed to help you acquire the attributes which you feel are vital to your success in such key events as applying for a crucial bank loan, making a pivotal business call, or interviewing for a lucrative contract, to mention just a few.

In exercises such as this, it is helpful to tap into the personal characteristics of someone who epitomizes those qualities you desire for yourself—an Ideal Model, so to speak. This script, therefore, calls for you to summon the image of an actual or imaginary "hero" or "heroine" you would like to emulate in critical circumstances such as a climactic meeting with an important prospect, the setting of this particular scenario. Adapt this exercise to your own important event.

Start by putting aside some uninterruptible time. Make yourself comfortable. Take a Signal Breath, then allow your breathing to settle into a soothing rhythm. Give yourself permission to take all the time you need for your body and mind to come to a level of relaxation that is just right for you today.

When you are ready, invite a picture to form of the situation that requires your self-confidence. The outcome of this activity or undertaking is critical to your success in working alone. To make the scene as real as possible, to bring it vividly to life in your mind, take a few moments to flesh out the details of this environment . . . take notice of the shapes, colors, and textures of the scene. What time of day does it appear to be? Do you hear any sounds? Are there any smells you can identify? Does anything else about the image make an impression on you? What is the mood, the atmosphere of this scene today? Is it friendly? Forbidding?

Now imagine your ideal model coming into this setting to accomplish the task, to meet the challenge that is so important. This person, real or imaginary, embodies all the qualities vital to the successful outcome of this critical event. (For the sake of narrative clarity, let's say the Ideal Model is a woman.)

Again, the more details you can flesh out, the more vivid the scene will be in your mind. What is she wearing? What expression is on her face? What is she doing with her hands? Study her closely as she enters . . . how she greets the prospective client. Notice her tone of voice. Watch and listen intently as the interview progresses. Note whatever she says or does that appears to help her cause.

Then, after you've observed the scene as you might a movie on the screen . . . and learned as much as you can in that manner . . . move *inside* this ideal person and *become* her. Now you're inside her body . . . look out through her eyes . . . feel the self-confidence radiate through your whole being . . . *know* what you need to know . . . and have what you need to have to pull this important thing off . . . sense how it feels to sit with poise . . . move dynamically . . . speak with strength and clarity . . . listen intelligently . . . respond alertly . . . state your case eloquently . . . handle yourself impressively . . . and emerge victorious. Envision any other qualities you consider important to the success of this event. See them personified in this heroic model.

While you're in your ideal model, exult in how good self-confidence feels, notice where in your body the self-confidence seems to be centered. Is there a source point from which it seems to flow? Notice that you can actually elevate the intensity of the good feelings you experience simply by thinking about them. Experiment with increasing your sense of confidence. Feel it pouring out of you into the room, into your home, into the universe.

Now, while you have that sense of supreme self-confidence, form an "anchor." Perform a simple, inconspicuous action such as crossing your arms or crossing two fingers or touching the palm of a hand to your cheek. But actually *do* it . . . know as you perform this simple action that you are pairing your intense feelings of self-confidence with this physical cue . . . know that whenever you would like to return to these feelings of calmness and competence, you can do so by using the "anchor" to access them.

Hold the anchor while you savor the feelings for as long as you choose . . . then release it . . . and whenever you are ready, move out of the image of your Ideal Model. In closing with this scene, thank the participants, especially your Ideal Model for helping you today . . . and gradually return to the here and now, knowing you can re-experience the personal confidence, eloquence, and poise simply by forming the anchor. Secure in that knowledge, come back to the here and now.

Paul Lambert is a licensed massage therapist whose office is a converted garage attached to his home. He had completed all the schooling and training required by the state licensing board and now was trying to build a practice in the face of considerable competition in his field.

Print advertising was necessary, Lambert knew, but in itself insufficient. He felt he needed to make his name and face known to doctors and therapists—those important professionals who could refer clients to him. Accomplishing this end meant offering free seminars to educate potential referral sources on the benefits of his type of massage.

But he dreaded the whole idea. Aside from his distaste for public speaking, his confidence and self-esteem, once buoyed by his successful training experiences, had been eroded by the depressingly slow trickle of clients to his door. Still, he knew that in order to achieve a successful practice he'd have to overcome his reluctance in marketing his special skills through the forum of public seminars. In his desperation he turned to guided imagery.

Lambert had no difficulty selecting his Ideal Model: Jim Beazely, a fellow student in his massage therapy school who had once presented information to the rest of the class for an engaging hour. With his poise, wit, and easy presence, Beazely had quickly captivated the other students.

During the imagery exercise, Eric was able to vividly recall the details and nuances of Beazely's masterful presentation on that memorable day. Lambert moved into his classmate's form and discovered how it felt, from the inside, to address a roomful of people confidently and effectively.

He learned to relax, to move and speak naturally, to use humor to drive home key points, to be warm and friendly, yet thoroughly professional. Satisfied he had accurately captured his mentor's techniques and skills, Lambert anchored them by folding his arms across his chest. As he prepared for his first presentation, a monthly meeting of the local Counseling and Therapy Association, Lambert practiced using his anchor.

His guided imagery exercise paid off beautifully. As he was introduced to the large gathering, he once again anchored his poise and confidence, and then proceeded to give an outstanding presentation. Several therapists approached him afterwards, expressing their interest in working with him, and he received three referrals from that group alone.

Script #5: Tapping Your Wellspring

All of us, whether we work from home or not, can benefit tremendously by taking some time on a regular basis to tap into that pool of inner resources from which we draw. Deep inside each of us is an inexhaustible wellspring of raw talent, creative energy, vital passion, and limitless strength.

It is there, as surely as we draw breath, but access to our inner source of happiness and vitality may have been sealed off. Or maybe the path to it has become overgrown and obstructed from lack of use. Whether you work from home because that is your heart's desire or because it is the least objectionable option in your life right now, you need to replenish your passion, spirit, and purpose in life constantly.

This imagery will ease the passage and access to your wellspring. No longer will it be a major pilgrimage but, instead, a regular, refreshing, enjoyable, even irresistible visit to your storehouse of precious internal resources.

Begin by allowing yourself 15 or 20 minutes of uninterrupted time . . . settling now into your body . . . making yourself comfortable . . . loosening tight clothing . . . taking a Signal Breath: exhaling strongly, inhaling deeply, exhaling strongly again . . . letting go the outside world . . . relaxing your muscles completely . . . easing your joints . . . melting into yourself . . . releasing . . . softening into your body . . . everything soft . . . your belly soft . . . your breathing soft . . . opening yourself . . . not trying . . . not making anything happen . . . just allowing . . . trusting your body and mind to find the rhythmic breathing that is perfect for you . . . here . . . and now . . . as you drift . . . allowing each circular cycle of breath to invite you deeper . . . closer to the level of relaxation and comfort that is just right for you today . . . but not hurrying . . . taking all the time you want . . . taking all the time you need.

When you are ready, imagine yourself at a trailhead. You know the wellspring of your inner strengths and talents lie at the end of this trail. But there's terrain to cross before you reach the headwaters of your creativity and passion. Allow the landscape to unfold. Let it become whatever it wants to be . . . mountain or mesa, canyon or desert, forest or tundra . . . for you to traverse in order to replenish yourself from your deepest source.

As you begin your journey, drink in the surroundings . . . What colors, shapes and textures catch your eye? . . . Is anything moving in the landscape? . . . What time is it? . . . How's the weather? . . . Does the air smell sweet? . . . Do you hear sounds along the way? . . . What do you feel on your skin? . . . what do you feel inside of you as you move?

There may be some difficulties for you on this journey. Let them come. Notice exactly what obstructs your way . . . What distractions are trying to lure you off your course? . . . What terrain or weather impedes your progress? . . . Note you are meeting each challenge with commitment and determination.

Tell yourself, since this journey is taking place in your imagination, it doesn't have to be an exhausting struggle. You can use whatever methods work best to get you where you want to go. Become a soaring eagle . . . a feather wafted on gentle currents of air . . . or run like the wind, effortlessly and strong, on soft forest trails . . . becoming whatever you want to become . . . doing whatever you need to do . . . drawing closer to your destination . . . drawn steadily by the awareness of how important it is to reach your wellspring . . . how vital it is to your happiness and success that you tap your inner resources.

Closing in on the source now . . . seeing the water surge from the ground, clear and pure . . . an inexhaustible, ever-replenishing supply of life-restoring, spirit-nourishing energy.

Drinking deeply from the wellspring now . . . feeling the vitality course through your body . . . bathing every cell of your being with quiet strength . . . grounding you in power . . . washing you with creativity . . . charging your intellect and emotions . . . cleansing and restoring your mind and spirit.

Taking it into the very marrow of your bones . . . letting it suffuse your entire being . . . satiating you with the clear, stable passion that is your core energy . . . feeling it course and radiate through every pore of your body . . . giving yourself as much time as you want at this sacred site . . . exulting in your power . . . perhaps performing a small ritual of gratitude.

When you are ready, in preparation for leaving, notice the place in your body where the wellspring energy feels strongest, where its core seems to reside in you . . . knowing all you need to do to reconnect with these inner resources is to focus on that touchstone in your body . . . knowing you have found the way and marked the spot . . . knowing you can return to your wellspring any time . . . to replenish your energy . . . to recharge your determination . . . to nourish your talents.

Now, beginning the journey back . . . coming again to this time and place . . . easing into the here and now . . . bringing with you all you need to remember from this experience . . . feeling content and comfortable . . . returning at peace with your mind and body . . . returning alert and refreshed . . . returning renewed.

Werner Kirschner makes beautiful handcrafted furniture. He is a consummate artist who brilliantly uses his medium of wood to create rockers, tables, dressers, and chests. Every piece evolves as a work of art, each unique, turning the special qualities of the rich wood into magnificent function and form.

His breathtaking creations are born of remarkable energy and inspiration that flow, of course, from an internal source. But there are times when he feels depleted, listless, uninspired. During such times, Kirschner has found, a guided imagery trip to his wellspring invariably helps. There, he is always joined by his great-grandfather, whom he never met in real life, an Austrian cello maker of high repute. At the wellspring, the two craftsmen soak in a natural hot spring. In their time together, Kirschner reminds himself of the artistic heritage that sustains him. He asks his venerable ancestor for encouragement and support. Occasionally he solicits advice on artistic and technical problems. All the while, he releases his tiredness, absorbs creativity, and replenishes energy for the demanding solitary work he loves.

PICK UP THIS MARVELOUS TOOL AND USE IT

You've now read five guided imagery scripts and an example of how each was used effectively by a homeworker. But the scripts are simply tools, says Pingree—potent instruments of personal discovery and growth for those with the trust, confidence, and willingness to use them.

"Certainly homeworkers can prevail without guided imagery," she concedes. "These techniques are by no means a prerequisite for thriving and prospering as a homeworker. Just reading the scripts won't attain your goals any more than reading about hammers will drive a nail. You have to pick up the tool and use it, perhaps repeatedly.

"Tune in to yourself through guided imagery," urges Pingree. "Listen. Respond and grow. The key to your success is your innate ability to improvise and create. When you learn to pay attention to yourself, to trust your intuitive images, and to treat them with the awareness and compassion they deserve, you will find you have a lifelong resource that will support and guide you on your exciting journey to self-fulfillment."

CHAPTER TWELVE

DEVELOPING

SURVIVAL SKILLS:

WHAT IT TAKES

TO BE "ON YOUR OWN"

"They endured." It's the last line of William Faulkner's *The Sound and the Fury*. "Endurance for one moment more" is how mountaineers of the Caucasus define heroism. One moment more—for as long as it takes. "To endure," wrote William Thackeray, "is greater than to dare."

It is endurance, above all, that marks the survivor. And for business psychologist Al Siebert, author of *The Survivor Personality*, "survivor" and "homeworker" are synonymous terms.

Siebert is uniquely qualified to make the equation because he has been a member of both groups since 1972. That was the year, he recalls, when a city inspector appeared as his door to demand a $25 fee for a municipal business license. A cranky neighbor had reported him to the city for working at his house. In addition, Siebert, internationally recognized for his research on survivor traits, has operated a home-based business since 1986.

"It takes a survivor personality to run a successful home-based business," he says bluntly. "To work from home is to survive in the truest sense of the word. It means drawing frequently on those pivotal personal traits that distinguish individuals who consistently pull through in the face of challenge and adversity."

THE MOST IMPORTANT TRAIT
HOME ALONERS POSSESS

"The most salient feature of the survivor's personality," observes researcher Edward E. Leslie, author of *Desperate Journeys, Abandoned Souls*, "is resilient, absolute determination. It is purposeful resolve. This trait is manifest in nearly every survivor narrative."

"They are able," summed up Virgil, "who *think* they are able."

Courage, ingenuity, optimism, humor, and flexibility also play a part in survival. But in the end, it is tenacity of will, indefatigable spirit, that forges survivors.

"We learn from them that adversity can be overcome by perseverance and ingenuity," says Leslie, that "we can endure and even triumph. These lessons may be absorbed in moments of serenity and contemplation and lie dormant until they are needed. Then they buoy us up."

The Difference Is Mental

Why, asks *OMNI* writer Janel Bladow about castaways at sea, does one person survive while another perishes? "Who hangs in there, it turns out, isn't determined by age, physical stamina, or experience," Bladow concludes.

"Although one would expect people who are fitter and more seaworthy to be the best candidates to make it back alive, the mind, that great trickster, isn't ruled by logic."

The difference lies in mental toughness rather than physical strength, believes Dr. William Zieverink, former chief of psychiatry at Cedar Hills Hospital in Portland, Oregon. "Survivors have a strong faith in themselves," says Zieverink. "Giving in to a sense of abandonment, means giving up. Survivors don't give up."

"Nurture the belief that you can *learn*, that you can *do* whatever it takes to succeed," Siebert exhorts homeworkers. "Know in your heart you can surmount all obstacles in your way." Siebert himself started his own business rather than give up on himself.

"The millions of people starting home-based businesses confirm my belief that a new breed of worker is emerging in our culture," says Siebert. "Because of their survivor traits, these extremely productive individuals are providing a higher value to themselves and to society by doing self-created, self-fulfilling work instead of routinely performing jobs thought up by others. These are highly flexible, keenly motivated, fiercely independent people, committed to service, constantly learning, and getting better and better at what they do."

Why are homeworkers succeeding in such vast numbers?

Although they differ as individuals, notes writer Bernard Gavzer, those who survive against tremendous odds have several things in common: 1) the pluck and courage to face up to almost anything; 2) spirituality; 3) irreverence, which includes an ability to laugh at oneself; and 4) a feeling of being chosen for an important mission.

A Passion for Life

Along with tenacity, a sturdy belief system, self-deprecating humor, come-what-may grit, and a sense of real purpose in life, survivors tend to be more resilient, enterprising, adaptable to change, ready to take the initiative, and willing to learn from their mistakes. They are distinguished by their fervor and zeal.

Survivors are passionate about themselves and the things they do. They believe they really count in life. They believe they make a difference, that what they do matters in the grand scheme of things.

These are the qualities and traits of people on their own.

ON YOUR OWN, BUT NOT ALONE

For some homeworkers, the key to surviving is the simple realization that being on your own doesn't mean having to be alone.

"One of the best things that happened to me in regard to working for myself and all the issues that entailed was finding out I was far from alone," says professional organizer Sue Hurlbut.

"What I thought was my totally unique idea for a business turned out to be one that others had acted on as well. That realization opened up a world of opportunity to me."

She didn't see competitors in her peers. She didn't see a weakening of her ideas because others had experienced them also. Instead, she saw power in numbers.

"I saw the opportunity to become better and stronger, the chance to build a better business by interacting with others who have the same enthusiasm and zeal for our emerging industry of professional organizing," says Hurlbut.

"I saw I wasn't alone at all, far from it. For me and everyone else on their own, there's a national association of people out there with similar aspirations and needs, struggling with the same issues and challenges. We can all help each other."

Trade and professional associations give people who work alone the opportunity to have their hands held, and to hold the hands of others like them.

"We can draw from a collective passion because we share a common dream," says Hurlbut. "We understand what each other is trying to achieve because we all speak the same language. And so we can help each other accomplish much more than we can do by ourselves."

There's a flotilla of industry groups out there to help keep you afloat. They're just waiting to welcome you. Instructional associations such as Toastmasters International, a public speaking organization that helps build business and interpersonal skills while giving members the opportunity to interact with sympathetic people outside the realm of their particular struggles.

Support organizations for home-based entrepreneurs are springing up all over the country. They provide a forum for homeworkers to encourage and help each other succeed, apart but together.

"They give us a break from our daily preoccupations and worries," says Hurlbut. "They allow us to learn about overcoming our weaknesses without having to confess to them. They give us a podium for imparting inspiration and instruction—and for receiving it.

"Interacting with others just like us at luncheons, seminars, and workshops can provide a wealth of ideas, inspiration, and support. The psychic energy once garnered from co-workers is available in the more-focused venue of association meetings. The best way to survive on our own is to reach out and thrive with others."

NINE ESSENTIAL STRENGTHS

What distinguishes those who thrive on their own from those who don't?

According to Siebert, their key strengths include:

1. *Ability to learn from experience.* Survivors become "life smart" by finding lasting answers in the trying, difficult things that happen to them.

By retaining a childlike curiosity, by questioning constantly, by trusting their feelings, by being willing to experiment with life, and to make mistakes—even to look foolish provided they learn from them—they develop an increasingly accurate understanding of the world around them. This hard-earned understanding, in turn, refines their coping skills and talents.

Laid off when the advertising agency he worked for lost three major clients, Pat Mahoney wondered what he would do with his esoteric blend of creative-technical-managerial skills. But only briefly. "Not to worry," he assured himself. "You'll land on your feet. You're a survivor." And he did.

Mahoney started a small, profitable business selling the kinds of ads that are flashed onto movie theater screens before the show begins. His current clientele consists of neighborhood business owners who find Mahoney's type of affordable, close-to-home advertising perfectly suited to their specialized promotional needs.

"I simply took what I knew and applied it to another 'theater' of life," he says with a bemused twinkle in his eyes. "I'm creative and capable. I know that as a fact, the way I know the sun will rise tomorrow. I'm not cocky, just confident. I never worried that I wouldn't find a new way to support myself."

Traditionally, children and young adults learn by sitting in classrooms, studying textbooks, then taking tests. In the school of life, it's the opposite. First you take the test, then you learn the lesson—if you're smart, that is. Survivors learn from the tests life hands them. And they fare exceedingly well.

2. *Mental and emotional flexibility.* They have an internal "biphasic mode of adjustment." That's a fancy phrase for one's physical, mental, and emotional ability to approach, as well as to withdraw, from any given situation.

They can be optimistic and pessimistic, self-critical and self-confident, assured and doubtful, trusting and suspicious, selfish and unselfish—in fact, all at the same time. And because they can be both, they choose to respond in one way or the other, depending on the circumstances and the moment.

As an emergency room nurse at a sprawling medical center, Carla Webb was admired for her unfailing optimism and cheerfulness. She considered it part of her job—expecting the best from everyone around her and usually getting it. Her co-workers considered it a joy and a privilege to work with her.

When Webb went into private nursing, however, she found herself becoming increasingly wary of others. "I'd always been a highly optimistic person," she says, "and it bothered me that I was developing a pessimistic attitude, thinking negative thoughts, always on the lookout for potential problems.

"But I found it was part and parcel of being in business for myself, that I now have to be concerned with not being misled or lied to or cheated because my livelihood depends on it. I now have to be aware of the worst in people, as well as the best.

She laughs, then adds, "I'm still a highly optimistic person. I just have to be much more selective about it."

Survivors make their choices willingly. They exercise their options daringly. They act instead of react. Nonsurvivors are rigid, locked in, tipped out of balance in one direction—either not optimistic enough to risk or so optimistic they risk too much.

3. *Empathy*. This uniquely human survival skill allows them to recognize and understand how others feel without necessarily feeling the same way.

From their empathy flows a strong desire, even a passion, to make things all right for themselves and for everyone else. It's a quality that makes survivors so good in a service capacity. They're firmly in touch with their customers' and clients' feelings and genuinely want to please or satisfy them.

Over the years, Joan Chun, a secretary at a large industrial firm, had earned herself quite a reputation as a shopper for corporate executives. Busy employees who needed a gift on short notice had learned they could ask her to pick up a present for them during her lunch hour and she always came through for them in stunning fashion. Chun had exquisite taste, a fashion designer's eye for colors, and a bird dog's instinct for great buys. She always returned with a wonderful gift.

It was inevitable, therefore, that she would form her own personal shopping service, charging a fee for a task she'd once done for nothing. Chun set up a one-person shop on the ground floor of a large downtown office building and has done exceedingly well. "I saw a need," she says, "and I filled it."

Asked why she's good at what she does, Chun replies simply, "I'm a people person. I seem to have a sixth sense for what others like. I know how to talk to people. Companies and individuals in a service capacity must have this sixth sense.

"Call it empathy or sensitivity or consumer awareness or whatever you like, but companies and individuals in the business of catering to the public must have this quality or they will fail."

In the case of business people, professionals, and entrepreneurs, the synergistic drive that distinguishes survivors is a motivating principle in their lives. It manifests itself in the high quality of the services and products they are motivated to develop and provide the world.

4. *Positive outlook.* They anticipate and overcome obstacles to their success. They learn from difficulties and past failures. They're adept at thinking in positive ways to surmount negative developments. And they adjust their actions to ensure success.

Earl Flynn earns his living by washing office building windows. He works out of his home and secures most of his work by bidding on contracts. It's a highly competitive business in the medium-size city in which he lives and he's not always successful despite being an independent contractor without the overhead of running a company. But he learns from every job he loses.

Recently, Flynn bid on a contract to wash the windows of a large office building in an industrial mall. After submitting his bid, he was called in by the building manager and told that his price was virtually identical to another competitor. "I'd like to give the work to you," the manager informed him, "but I need a reason to do so. Can you see your way clear to lowering your price?"

Flynn was torn on how to respond. He could refuse and lose the work or acquiesce and fail to realize a fair profit, both of which he'd done in the past. And for him, both were unsatisfactory outcomes. Flynn proposed an alternative. If the manager would allow him to wash the windows over the period of two weekends instead of during a working week, he would lower his price. He could do so and make up the difference, Flynn explained, because the preparatory work of covering cars with tarps and accommodating pedestrian traffic would be eliminated on a weekend. The manager acquiesced and Flynn got the contract.

Survivors have a talent for serendipity. They convert challenge into opportunity. Hit with a setback, they see it as temporary and surmountable. When something goes wrong, they try to understand why and do things differently the next time.

Knocked off track, they instinctively ask themselves, "How can I turn this around? Why is it a blessing in disguise that this happened? How can I make it pay off for me?" And they react accordingly, often emerging victorious.

6. *Results orientation.* They're good at what they do, sometimes *too* good. Because of their ability to grasp situations quickly, to remedy unsatisfactory situations as quickly as possible, they feel frustrated when those in charge don't understand their proposed solutions or won't follow their suggestions. What they do, how they do it, and *why* all have to make complete sense to them.

Judy Warshaw admits she's more comfortable dealing with "things" than "people." She has better luck with the former than the latter, she admits ruefully. As quality control manager for a manufacturing firm that produced carbon cartridges for computer printers, she yearned to be on her own instead of running a department with seven employees.

Also, as a socially conscious, environmentally concerned individual, she was bothered by the waste factor built into the product her company turned out. The printer cartridges were designed to be replaced with new ones when they ran out of carbon, at a per-unit cost of $95.

Warshaw wound up creating a business to recycle the cartridges for customers. She arranged to pick up the units when they were empty, modify several inner parts, refill the cartridges with carbon, and return them to the customers at a cost of $50—almost half the cost of a new item.

"My new business provides me satisfaction on a number of levels," she says, "but I'm most pleased that my technological ability allowed me to provide an alternative to mindless waste for my customers and the community.

Survivors have an overriding desire is to make things work well at all costs. It's why they're often accused of "making waves" or not being "team players." Because their greatest luxury is the freedom to do whatever has to be done without interference, eventually their only course is to venture out on their own.

6. *Self-confidence.* They trust themselves because they can experience multiple, often conflicting feelings while their inner gyroscope keeps them centered. They're able to say, "I blew it." Or "That didn't work. Let's go back to square one."

Lloyd Hunt was a savings and loan executive specializing in small business loans. When a large financial institution bought out his firm and promptly eliminated his job, Hunt promptly became a consultant to entrepreneurs and small firms seeking venture capital.

"I'm much happier now," he says. "Somehow, I knew this day would come and I almost welcomed it. Funny thing is, I feel far more secure than I ever did working for someone else. Maybe it's because I have myself to rely on now instead of other people. I like it much better this way. I'll sink or swim on my own merits, not someone else's. That in itself is worth everything to me."

Survivors are able to see what's happening instead of what they merely wish was happening. And they deal with the consequences.

7. *Willingness to experiment.* Because it's highly important to them that things "go" well, they're willing to experiment with different ways and means in order to find out what works best for them. They're more interested in results than who happens to be right. They self-manage their learning beyond the scope and advice of the so-called experts. They're not bothered by what they see and think not fitting in what others see and think.

As a division manager with a high-tech firm, Jim Borland had the uncanny knack of seeing the big picture and all the little parts it took to make the picture complete. He always had a clear vision of everything that needed to be done, major and minor, in order for his manufacturing arm to function at peak capacity.

"I saw my role then," he says, "as a key facilitator—informing, instructing, encouraging, motivating, getting others to get the maximum production and best quality out of the assembly equipment they were running." Nothing's really changed for Borland as a technical consultant except that he makes more money. What drives him as an independent contractor, he says, is what drove him to excellence as a corporate manager—the overwhelming need for everything to work well.

Survivors have a strong sense of when things are working well and when they're not that doesn't come from memorized rules or techniques. It springs from an inner awareness of nature's principles and laws. When things aren't working well, they feel an urge to make improvements. And they rebel against efforts to thwart their effectiveness.

Because of this synergistic compulsion, survivors tend to be tough, decisive, assertive, multifaceted, competent people. As a result, they're usually highly formidable competitors.

8. *Adaptability*. They can adapt to the changes and developments in the world around them.

After 30 years as a government employee, most of that time spent in the ranks of upper management, Jim Dowd embarked on a second career as woodworker, specializing in home remodeling. Long accustomed to telling others what to do, he now had to take orders. He had to ask questions, listen carefully, and respond exactly to what his clients wanted done. "It took quite an attitude adjustment," Dowd says sheepishly.

Though it may be extremely hard at times, survivors are able to adjust their desires, attitude, and behavior to exigencies of success and survival.

9. *Playfulness*. Personified by Hawkeye Pierce, the character played by Alan Alda in the popular TV series, M*A*S*H, survivors use playfulness to maintain their emotional stability and professional effectiveness in the midst of chaos, uncertainty, and huge potential loss.

Tom Sullivan, an independent printing rep, is probably more successful than he deserves to be for a reason he readily acknowledges: "I'm easy to do business with." Blessed with an irrepressible sense of humor, he's seldom turned away when he drops in on a client. More than his charm and wit, however, is his grace under fire. When things go wrong, it's a pleasure to deal with him because of his unfailing pleasantness and unflappable equanimity.

"Whatever the problem," he says, "the first thing I do is try to defuse the tense situation. The last thing distraught clients need is for their suppliers to get upset and defensive too. Right off, I promise to do whatever's necessary to remedy their problem, and I try to assure them in a low-key, humorous manner. When the crisis is over, that's what they remember—how I made them laugh under fire, when they absolutely wanted to kill me."

"Playing" keeps survivors in firm contact with what's happening around them. It helps them take the onus off threatening situations. It enables them to remain calm in challenging circumstances by maintaining an imperturbable attitude: "This situation is my toy. It doesn't scare me. I can play with it." It helps them maintain their equanimity under great stress.

People who can play are able to see the humor in the human condition, to appreciate the comic turns and twists of destiny. They're able to view life from other perspectives than their own. The ability to be playful in business stratagems can be a potent prowess.

TAKE PRIDE IN SUCCEEDING ON YOUR OWN

Stretching his lanky frame, Siebert gazes from the deck of his home on the Columbia River that also serves as his national base of operations. "Take pride in being a survivor, in working alone," he exhorts his fellow homeworkers. "Tell yourself you're independent, a maverick, maybe even a misfit, whether through circumstance or choice.

"But whether you choose to work alone or do it out of necessity, remind yourself, 'I have to be completely responsible for what I do. If I fail, I won't blame anyone else. I'll learn from my mistakes, I'll build on my failures. And I'll succeed the next time. Or the next. But I *will* succeed. Because I'm a *survivor!*'"

Celebrate Yourself

You *are* one, you know. On your own. Wholly dependent on *your* grit, *your* determination, *your* stamina, *your* skills.

You're tough inside, where it counts.

You know that emotional strength more than physical endurance determines who will succeed and who will fail.

You're willing to risk. And live with the consequences. Because you know that failing won't cripple you. But not trying surely will.

You operate on the daily premise that nothing is certain but change, that a lifetime of self-denial doesn't guarantee a secure, content retirement, so you'd rather fail on the side of exuberance than caution.

You've learned that laughter is an effective way of dealing with a weird and frightening world.

You know that most of the trouble in life is caused by people who take themselves too seriously. So you try not to do the same, believing that both the world and you will benefit from your humility.

Steven Callahan, a naval architect who spent 76 days in the Atlantic on a 5-1/2-foot inflatable raft and lived to tell about it, dedicated his book *Adrift* to you:

"To people everywhere who know, have known, or will know suffering, desperation, or loneliness."

As a solitary striver you'll become well acquainted with at least two out of the three. But you'll be around to celebrate yourself for a very long time.

"Light the candles and pour the red wine," suggests *Esquire* writer Daniel Halpern. "Raise your glass in honor of yourself. The company is the best you'll ever have."

Here's to you!

Here's to us all!

On our own.

BIBLIOGRAPHY

Achterberg, Jeanne, *Imagery in Healing* (Boston: New Science Library, 1985).

Ansberry, Clare and O'Boyle, Thomas F., "Voices of a Generation Fear for the Status of American Dream," *The Wall Street Journal*, August 13, 1992.

Armstrong, Larry, "Who Needs a Desk When You've Got a Lap?" *Business Week*, March 18, 1991.

Austin, Nancy, "Movers and Shakers: The New Breed," *Working Woman*, May 1992.

Ball, Aimee Lee, "Life After Greed," *Mademoiselle*, June 1991.

Barnard, Jeff, "Rogue River Retreat Gives Space and Time to Writers," *The Oregonian*, June 5, 1994.

Barrier, Michael, "How a Dallas Consultant Helps Managers Attack the Paper Piled On Their Desks," *Nation's Business*, January 1992.

Barry, Dave, "The Pleasures and Pitfalls of Working At Home," *The Oregonian*, May 10, 1992.

Begley, Adam, "Case of the Brooklyn Symbolist." *The New York Times Magazine*, August 30, 1992.

Bernikow, Louise, *Alone In America* (New York: Harper & Row, 1986).

Black, Pam, "A Home Office That's Easier On the Eyes—and the Back," *Business Week*, August 17, 1992.

Bladow, Janel, "Swept Away." *Omni*, September 1990.

Block, Jean Libman, "Working at Home," *Good Housekeeping*, March 1991.

Braus, Patricia, "Homework," *American Demographics*, August 1993.

Brazelton, T. Berry, "How Active Is Hyperactive?" *Family Circle*, May 12, 1992.

Brody, Jane E., "Personal Health." *The New York Times*, September 30, 1992.

Bry, Adelaide, *Visualization* (New York: Harper & Row, 1979).

Burns, David D., *The Feeling Good Handbook* (New York: William Morrow & Co., Inc., 1989).

Burros, Marian, "Tipper Gore Winning a Personal Campaign," *The New York Times*, July 7, 1993.

Calem, Robert E., "Working at Home, for Better or Worse," *The New York Times*, April 18, 1993.

Callahan, Steven, *Adrift: Seventy-Six Days Lost at Sea* (Boston: Houghton Mifflin, 1986).

Campbell, Bruce, "Home Work," *Working Woman*, June 1982.

Castro, Laura L., "Managers Declare Independence to Run Businesses From Their Personal Utopias," *The Wall Street Journal*, September 3, 1991.

Chien, Philip, "The Frontiers of Space," *Compute*, September 1992.

Churbuck, David C. and Young, Jeffrey S., "The Virtual Workplace," *Forbes*, November 23, 1992.

Church, Foster, "The New Commute," *The Oregonian*, July 18, 1994.

Cronin, Anne, "This Is Your Life, Generally Speaking," *The New York Times*, July 26, 1992.

Crosby, Bill, "56 Square Feet of Maximum Efficiency," *Sunset*, February 1992.

Cunningham, Scott, and Porter, Alan L., "Communication Networks," *The Futurist*, January/February 1992.

Cutter, Blayne, "Getting Ahead In Slippers," *American Demographics*, February 1990.

Davidson, Margaret, "If You Want to Work at Home," *Good Housekeeping*, January 1992.

Dennis, Jeffery P., "Top Ten Time-Wasters," *The Writer*, April 1992.

Diamond, Deborah Beroset, "A Great Place to Work," *Ladies Home Journal*, May 1992.

Diesenhouse, Susan, "In a Shaky Economy, Even Professionals Are 'Temps,'" *The New York Times*, May 16, 1993.

Dunne, John Gregory, "Sweet Liberty," *Esquire*, March 1987.

Eberstadt, Fernanda, "A Gathering of Household Gods," *House & Garden*, June 1992.

Edmondson, Brad, "Remaking a Living," *Utne Reader*, July/August 1991.

Edwards, Paul and Sarah, *Working From Home: Everything You Need to Know About Living and Working Under the Same Roof* (Los Angeles: Jeremy P. Tarcher, Inc., 1987).

Espindle, Michael D., "1992 Survey Results," *Home Office Computing*, September 1992.

Everett, Martin, "TV or Not TV? Mental Calisthenics for the Phone," *Sales & Marketing Management*, December 1992.

Exeter, Thomas G., "The Next Step Is Called GIS," *American Demographics Desk Reference*, May 1992.

Farmanfarmaian, Roxane, "Worksteading," *Psychology Today*, November 1989.

Faulkner, William, *The Sound and the Fury*, (New York: Random House, 1984).

Fezler, William, *Imagery for Healing, Knowledge and Power* (New York: Simon & Schuster Inc., 1990).

_____, "Fighting Fire With Focus," *Psychology Today*, February 1993.

Fishel, Ruth, *The Journey Within* (Deerfield Beach: Health Communications, 1987).

Flaste, Richard, "Sidelined By Loneliness," *The New York Times Magazine*, April 28, 1991.

Forester, Tom, "The Myth of the Electronic Cottage," *Futures*, June 1988.

Forman, Andrew M. and Shiram, Ven, "The Depersonalization of Retailing: Its Impact on the Lonely Consumer," *Journal of Retailing*, Summer 1991.

Frakes, Mary, "Having It All," *Boston Magazine*, June 1991.

Fraser, Jill Andresky, "Conflicts in Resuming the Corporate Career," *The New York Times*, May 15, 1994.

Frerking, Beth, "Stay-At-Home Dads Isolated in No-Man's Land," *The Oregonian*, June 12, 1994.

Friedman, Dana, "The Juggling Act," *Working Mother*, April 1992.

Friedman, Rick, "In the Office—at Home: An Idea Is Catching On," *The Office*, April 1991.

Frohbieter-Mueller, Jo, *Stay Home and Mind Your Own Business* (White Hall, VA: Betterway Publications, 1987).

Gardner, Marilyn, "Craving Solitude In a Crowded World," *The Christian Science Monitor*, March 10, 1992.

Garfield, Charles A., *Peak Performers: The New Heroes of American Business* (New York, W. Morrow, 1986).

Gavzer, Bernard, "What Keeps Me Alive," *Parade*, January 31, 1993.

Gawain, Shakti, *Creative Visualization* (Berkeley: Whatever Publishing, 1978).

Geist, William, "Home Sick," *New York*, April 3, 1989.

Gite, Lloyd, "The Home-Based Executive," *Black Enterprise*, January 1991.

Glory, Blaise, "Managing Information Resources In a Telecommuting Environment," *Special Libraries*, Winter 1994.

Goleman, Daniel, "Holocaust Survivors Had Skills to Prosper," *The New York Times*, October 6, 1992.

Goleman, Daniel and Gurin, Joel, edited by, *Mind/Body Medicine* (New York: Consumer Reports Books, 1993).

Goodman, Susan, "The Value of Solitude," *Current Health 2*, March 1992.

Greene, Melissa Fay, "A Writer's Life In a Household of Children," *Ms.*, May/June 1992.

Grimes, William, "Making a Virtue of Legwork," *The New York Times*, July 8, 1993.

Grunwald, Lisa, "Is It Time to Get Out?" *Esquire*, April 1990.

Hallam, Linda, "Working At Home," *Southern Living*, June 1991.

Halpern, Sue, *Migrations to Solitude* (New York: Pantheon Books, 1992).

Harris, Jean, *Marking Time: Letters from Jean Harris to Shana Alexander* (New York: Macmillan, 1992).

Hedrick, Lucy, *Five Days to an Organized Life* (New York: Dell, 1990).

Hill, Jim, "Business Cycle Taken Literally," *The Oregonian*, May 12, 1993.

Hollahan, David, "Leave Me (Home) Alone," *The Wall Street Journal*, May 13, 1993.

Holtz, Herman, *The Complete Work-at-Home Companion* (Rocklin, CA: Prima Publishing & Communications, 1990).

Hotch, Ripley, "All the Comforts of a Home Office," *Nation's Business*, July 1993.

Hotch, Ripley, "Managing From a Distance," *Nation's Business*, February 1993.

_____, "How Do You Squeeze In a Home Workspace?" *Sunset*, March 1991.

Howard, Bill, "Bringing It All Back Home," *Lear's*, February 1993.

Huber, Peter, "The Unbundling of America," *Forbes*, April 13, 1992.

Jones, Ted and McMillan, Pat, "Creative Home Offices," *Home Mechanix*, March 1991.

Jong, Erica, "Writers Dwell in Dreams of Houses and Houses of Dreams," *The New York Times,* December 30, 1993.

Kahl, Rick, "At Home In the Office," *Skiing*, November 1991.

Kanarek, Lisa, "America's Most Disorganized Home Offices," *Home Office Computing*, August 1993.

Kanarek, Lisa, "Curing High Anxiety: 5 Days to An Organized Office," *Home Office Computing*, August 1992.

Katz, Donald R., "Hard Facts About the Home Office," *Esquire*, April 1990.

Kaufman, Michael T., "Notes From Underground Prove Rewarding to Author," *The New York Times*, January 13, 1993.

Keller, John J., "In 'Virtual Office,' High-Speed Lines Rule," *The Wall Street Journal*, May 17, 1993.

Kidd, Billy and McCluggage, "Secrets of Visualization," *Skiing*, March 1991.

Kiester Jr., Edwin and Kiester, Sally Valente, "Secrets of Straight-A Students," *Reader's Digest*, September 1992.

Kilborn, Peter T., "New Jobs Lack the Old Security In Time of 'Disposable Workers'," *The New York Times*, March 15, 1983.

Klotzburger, Katherine M., "I'll Stop Procrastinating Tomorrow," *Woman's Day*, September 22, 1992.

Kurtz, Theodore, "10 Reasons Why People Procrastinate," *Supervisory Management*, April 1990.

Lamb, Lynette, "The 21st-Century Office," *Utne Reader*, March/April 1994.

Lehmkuhl, Dorothy, *The Organizing Bible*. (Bloomfield, MI: Organizing Techniques, 1992).

Leimbach, Penton, "How to Get Organized," *Mother Earth News*, October/November 1992.

Leslie, Edward E., *Desperate Journeys, Abandoned Souls* (Boston: Houghton Mifflin, 1988).

____, "Let a Smile Be Your Umbrella," *The Oregonian*, June 1, 1994.

Lewis, Peter H., "More Home Workers and More Machines In Their Offices," *The New York Times*, May 24, 1992.

Liberman, Jacob, *Light, Medicine of the Future*, (Santa Fe: Bear & Co., 1991).

____, "Living Alone," *Mayo Clinic Health Letter*, September 1992.

Lohr, Steve, "Fewer Ties Are Bonding Workers to Corporations," *The New York Times*, August 14, 1992.

Lyall, Sarah, "Finding Silly Stuff In Ordinary Life," *The New York Times*, July 1, 1993.

_____, "Making a List and Checking It Twice," *Current Health 2*, January 1992.

Mahoney, Sarah, "A Restless Middle Age," *Adweek*, July 1, 1991.

Mansnerus, Laura, "Count to 10 and Pet the Dog," *The New York Times Magazine*, April 25, 1993.

Matthews, Anne, "The Campus Crime Wave," *The New York Times Magazine*, March 7, 1993.

Matthews-Simonton, Stephanie, *Getting Well Again* (Toronto: Bantam Books, 1980).

McCluggage, Denise, "Making Mental Movies," *Skiing*, February 1992.

McGarvey, Robert, "Picture Yourself a Winner," *Kiwanis*, October 1990.

McLaughlin, Patricia, "Boomers Discover Death Isn't Just for Other People," *The Oregonian*, June 12, 1994.

Meer, Ameena and Worth, James, "The Writer's Room," *Harper's Bazaar*, February 1992.

Middaugh, Susan L., "Why You Need Your Own Office," *The Writer*, August 1984.

Micheli, Robin, "Home Is Where the Office Is," *Money*, July 1988.

Mills, Miriam K., "SMR Forum: Teleconferencing—Managing the 'Invisible Worker'," *Sloan Management Review*, Summer 1984.

Nadel, Laurie with Haims, Judy and Stempson, Robert, *Sixth Sense: The Whole-Brain Book of Intuition, Hunches, Gut Feelings and Their Place in Your Every Day Life* (New York: Prentice Hall, 1990).

Noble, Barbara Presley, "Get a Life, They Said. And Did," *The New York Times*, May 10, 1992.

Oldenburg, Ray, *The Great Good Place* (New York: Paragon Books, 1989).

Oldham, John M. and Morris, Lois B., *Personality Self-Portrait* (New York: Bantam Books, 1991).

Olshan, Joseph, "The Company of Dogs," *The New York Times Magazine*, March 14, 1993.

O'Malley, Christopher, "The Well-Connected Office," *Popular Science*, October 1992.

O'Rourke, Kelly, "A Spell of Stormy Weather," *Cosmopolitan*, September 1990.

Patton, Phil, "The Virtual Office Becomes Reality," *The New York Times*, October 28, 1993.

Peck, M. Scott, *The Road Less Traveled: A New Psychology of Love, Traditional Values and Spiritual Growth* (New York: Simon & Schuster, 1978).

Peper, George, "Out-House Editors," *Golf*, July 1991.

Plummer, Joseph T., "Changing Values," *The Futurist*, January/February 1989.

Porges, Paul Peter, "The Pros and Cons of Working at Home," *New Choices*, July 1990.

Pouschine, Tatiana and Kripalani, Manjeet, "I Got Tired of Forcing Myself to Go to the Office," *Forbes*, May 25, 1992.

Powell, Barbara, *Good Relationships Are Good Medicine* (Emmaus, PA: Rodale Press, 1987).

Ramirez, Anthony, "It's a Bank. It's a Brain. No, It's Superphone," *The New York Times*, February 4, 1993.

Ranard, Ann, "How Not To Be a Worrywart," *McCall's*, September 1992.

Rinehart, Robert, "Setting Goals," *Women's Sports & Fitness*, January/February 1993.

Roha, Ronaleen R., "Call Your Own Shots," *Kiplinger's Personal Finance Magazine*, June 1992.

Roome, Hugh, "The Bright Spot," *Home Office Computing*, September 1992.

Rosen, Margery D., "All Alone," *Ladies' Home Journal*, April 1991.

Rosenblatt, Roger, "The Solitary Child," *Family Circle*, February 1, 1992.

Rossman, Martin L., *Healing Yourself* (New York: Pocket Books, 1989).

Rottenberger-Murtha, Kerry, "Q: Is the 'Virtual Office' a Viable Option?" *Sales & Marketing Management*, September 1993.

Sabath, Ann Marie, "Business Etiquette," *Sales & Marketing Management*, November 1991.

Samalin, Nancy with McCormick, Patricia, "Stop Dawdling!" *Parents*, November 1992.

Samuels, Mike and Samuels, Nancy, *Seeing With the Mind's Eye* (New York: Random House, 1975)

Schnumberger, Lynn, "It's for You, Mom!" *Parents*, March 1989.

Schreiber, Norman, "Home Is Where the Office Is," *Writer's Digest*, December 1991.

Schwartz, John and Tsiantar, Dody with Springen, Karen, "Escape From the Office," *Newsweek*, April 24, 1989.

Seal, Kathy, "On the Job," *Parenting*, May 1992.

Sheehy, Edna, *Start and Run a Profitable Home-Based Business* (British Columbia: Self-Counsel Press, 1990).

Shellenbarger, Sue, "Fathers (Not Managers) Know Best," *The Wall Street Journal*, September 12, 1991.

Shellenbarger, Sue, "Home Workers Are a Bunch of Slobs," *The Wall Street Journal*, December 15, 1993.

Shrieves, Linda, "Who Are You Calling Slacker, You Yahoo Yuppie?", *The Oregonian*, May 19, 1994.

Siebert, Al and Gilpin, Bernardine, *The Adult Student's Guide to Survival and Success* (Portland, OR: Practical Psychology Press, 1992).

Siebert, Al, *The Survivor Personality* (Portland, OR: Practical Psychology Press, 1993).

Simpson, James B., *Webster's II New Riverside Desk Quotations* (Boston: Houghton Mifflin, 1992).

Simpson, Mona, "The Writer's Room," *Harper's Bazaar*, February 1992.

_____, "Six Diverse Types of Home Office," *The Futurist*, November/December 1991.

Smith, Morris S., "Fund Manager Steps Off the Treadmill," *The New York Times*, May 31, 1992.

Spikol, Art, "There's No Place Like Home," *Writer's Digest*, March 1989.

Stanton, Michael, "Freelancing: Is It for You?" *Occupational Outlook Quarterly*, Winter 1990–91.

Stoddard, Alexandra, "Make Time to Do It Now!" *McCall's*, October 1990.

Stone, Hal and Winkelman, Sidra, *Embracing Our Selves* (San Rafael: New World Library, 1989).

Storr, Anthony, *Solitude: A Return To the Self* (New York: Ballantine Books, 1988).

Sullivan, Nick, "The Ultimate Home Office: The White House," *Home Office Computing*, February 1992.

Swetnam, Susan H., "Dining Out: A Solitary Sport," *Gourmet*, September 1991.

Taylor, Kate, "Simple Life of the Sea Beckons," *The Oregonian,* August 20, 1994.

Toffler, Alvin, *The Third Wave* (New York: William Morrow, 1980).

Ungerleider, Steven, "Visions of Victory," *Psychology Today*, July/August 1992.

Van Nevel, Franny, "92 Timesavers," *Woman's Day*, August 23, 1992.

Veciana-Suarez, Ana, "No Woman Is an Island (Unfortunately)," *The Oregonian*, June 6, 1994.

Viorst, Judith, "Home Alone," *Redbook*, September 1991.

Wallace, Don, "The Home Office High Wire," *Home Office Computing*, October 1993.

Watkins, Mary, *Waking Dreams* (Dallas: Spring Publications, 1984).

Webster, Harriet, "The Organized Child," *Working Mother*, February 1993.

Wenner, Jenn S., "Time to Stop Calling Them 'Generation X'," *Advertising Age*, October 4, 1993.

_____, "What's Wrong With My Child?" *Ladies' Home Journal*, April 1992.

Whitmyer, Claude and Rasberry, Salli and Phillips, Michael, *Running a One-Person Business* (Berkeley: Ten Speed Press, 1989).

Wiener, Leonard, "Your Home, the Office," *U. S. News & World Report*, September 26, 1988.

Wiesendanger, Betsy, "Home Is Where the Customer Is," *Sales & Marketing Management*, August 1992.

Winik, Lyric Wallwork, "We Want Our Kids to See Another Side of Life," *Parade Magazine*, May 15, 1994.

Woolley, Suzanne, "Turning Home, Sweet Home Into Office, Sweet Office," *Business Week*, October 10, 1988.

_____, "Work Spaces That Work," *Woman's Day*, June 23, 1992.

INDEX

A

Adrift (Callahan), 192
Adult Student's Guide to Survival and Success (Siebert), 93
Advertising Age, 5
Adweek, 5
Alone, Alive and Well (Powell), 105, 113
American Dream, the real, 9-11, 13
American Home Business Association, 143
anchor, guided imagery, 175-76
anxiety, control of, 29-30, 91
Anywhere But Here (Simpson), 109
Aquinas, Thomas, 9
Art of Psychotherapy, The (Storr), 18
Association of Home Businesses, 142

attention deficit hyperactivity disorder, 49

B

baby boomers, 5, 8
Ballard, J.G., 68
Barry, Dave, 115
Bennett, Alan, 67
Better Homes and Gardens, 48
Beyond Strength (Ungerleider), 154
BIS Strategic Decisions, 2
Bladow, Janel, 182
Block, Lawrence, 101
Borkovec, Tom, 23
Brandt, Barbara, 15
Bry, Adelaide, 157
Bureau of Labor Statistics, 8
Burns, David, 89

Burroway, Janet, 36, 97
Bush, George, 9
Business Journal, The, 9

C

Callahan, Steven, 192
Capote, Truman, 13
Castaneda, Carlos, 5
Cedar Hills Hospital, 182
checklists, 59, 96-97
children, working at home with, 135-52
Christensen, Kathleen, 146
City University of New York, 146
clutter, control of, 58, 61-63, 151-52
Cody, Robin, 108-09
Colistro, Frank, 28-31
Colorado State University, 157
Columbian Missourian, The, 9
compromise, importance of, 99-100
Creative Visualization (Gawain), 154

D

decompression, psychic, 146-50
Desperate Journeys, Abandoned Souls (Leslie), 182
downshifting, 5
downsizing, 9
dress codes, 766-77
Drucker, Peter, 91
Dragon's Milk (Fletcher), 141

E

Edwards, Paul and Sarah, 37, 100
Einstein, Albert, 161

"electronic cottage," 2, 6, 9
empathy, 186-87
Empire of the Sun (Ballard), 68
entrepreneurs, 7-9
environmental concerns, 9
Esquire, 146, 192
Essential Jung, The (Storr), 18

F

family, working at home with, 135-152
Farmanfarmaian, Roxane, 73, 75, 143, 145
fast starts, 33-40
Faulkner, William, 181
fear of failure, 47, 49, 116
Feeling Good Handbook, The (Burns), 89
firewalking, 162
Five Days to An Organized Life (Hedrick), 84
Fletcher, Jerry, 141-43
Fletcher, Susan, 141-43
flexibility, mental, emotional, 185-86
floor space, office, 133-34
Freud, Sigmund, 160
fun, importance of, 24, 118-19

G

Gallup poll, 5
Gavzer, Bernard, 183
Gawain, Shakti, 153-54
Getting Well Again (Matthews-Simonton), 158
Gibran, Kahlil, 89
Goveia, John, 55-57

Great Good Place, The
(Oldenburg), 115
Greene, Melissa Fay, 138
Greenfield, Charles, 161
Grown Ups (Merser), 107
guided imagery, 153-80
guilt, constructive, 15-16, 46, 89,
92

H

Halberstam, David, 69
Halpern, Daniel, 192
Halpern, Sue, 105
Harper's Bazaar, 67
Harvard University, 8
Hedrick, Lucy, 59, 84
Hermann Brain Dominance
Profiles, 146-47
Holland, Barbara, 107-08
Home Office Computing, 4, 144
Home-Based Business News, 9
homeworkers, types, 7
numbers, 2-9, 143
HTO Enterprises, 22
Hurlbut, Sue, 22-24, 36, 45-46,
54-55, 58-63, 87, 111-13, 123,
183-84
hygiene, importance of, 76-77

I

ideal model, 174-76
individuality, 25-32
inner guide, advisor, 160-80
inner self, 156-80
IRS considerations, 72
isolation, 103-21

J

Jong, Erica, 118
Jung, Carl, 160

K

Kansas State University, 145
Katz, Donald R., 146
Kidd, Billy, 155-56
Kierkegaard, Soren, 104
Klotzburger, Katherine, 83, 86
Knowlton, John, 9
Kogen, Ron, 15-16, 88-89, 92
Krantz, Judith, 67
Kristall, Alexandra, 128-29, 147
Kurtz, Theodore, 90

L

Lao-Tzu, 26
Landers, Ann, 67
Lemkuhl, Dorothy, 44-45, 59, 92-
93, 97, 128-29
Leslie, Edward E., 182
LINK Resources, 2-3, 143
Linklater, Richard, 88
loneliness, 103-21
Lost Father, The (Simpson), 109

M

Mahoney, Sarah, 5
Malamud, Bernard, 33
Malone, Karl, 154-55

Matthews-Simonton, Stephanie,
    158, 160
McLemore, Gene, 43-44, 97
measuring success, 50-51
Merser, Cheryl, 107, 121
microflow activities, 76
Mid-Atlantic Education Institute
Middaugh, Susan, 71-73
Migrations to Solitude (Halpern),
    105
Miller, Tom, 143
Mills, Miriam K., 76
Morgan, Ted, 104
motives for working alone, 4-10
mottoes, use of, 66, 97
Ms., 138

away from home, 70-75
equipment, 123-134
furniture, 123-134
importance of, 65-80, 118-19
lighting, 124-26
Oldenburg, Ray, 115
Olshan, Joseph, 116
OMNI, 182
*One's Company: Reflections on
    Living Alone* (Holland), 107
organization, 53-63
Organization Plus, 111
Organizing Bible, The,
    (Lemkuhl), 44
*Organizing for the Creative
    Person* (Lemkuhl), 128

N

Nadel, Laurie, 146-47
National Association of
    Professional Organizers, 92
National Speaker's Association,
    143
Never Cry Wolf (movie), 65
New Jersey Institute of
    Technology, 76
New York Times, The, 2, 36, 67,
    88, 118
Nicklaus, Jack, 153
Nicholas, Jonathan, 74
Niles, John, 6
North Carolina Central University,
    23

P

Paine Webber/Young & Rubicam
    Ventures, 8
Patton, Phil, 2-3
Pavlovian responses, 37-40, 92
Peak Performers (Greenfield), 161
Peck, M. Scott, 11-12, 89-90
Pekala, Ronald J., 162
Pennsylvania State University, 23
pets, benefits of, 39, 115-16
physical fitness, importance of, 57
Pingree, Patricia Megan, 27-28,
    119-20, 155-80
playfulness, 190-91
Plummer, Joseph, 8
Powell, Barbara, 105, 113
problem-solving, 11-12
procrastination, 81-101
procrastinators, types, 86-87
productivity, maximizing, 53-63
pros and cons, working alone, 17-
    18

O

occupations, homeworkers, 7
office:

psychic maintenance, repair, 25-32
Psychology Today, 73, 144, 154

R

relaxation techniques, 157-180
respect, importance of, 150
rewarding yourself, 51, 84, 94-97, 117
Rice, Frederick H., 145
Ricochet River (Cody), 109
right brain/left brain considerations, 128-30
rituals, use of, 43-44
Road Less Traveled, The (Peck), 11-12
Robinson, Elwood, 23
Rolling Stone, 5
Rosenblatt, Roger, 105
Rubenstein, Carin, 121

S

Sales and Marketing Management, 3
Saltzman, Amy, 4-5
saying no, 44-48
saying yes, 48-51
scripts, guided imagery, 163-80
self-discipline, 10-12, 41-51, 54
self-discovery, 12
self-motivation, 41-51
separating home from office, 65-80
Servan-Schreiber, Louis, 89
Shaver, Phillip, 121
Shellenbarger, Sue, 139, 152
Shorter Work-Time Group, 15

Shulman, Dean, 144
Siebert, Al, 93-94, 117, 181-83, 185-91
signal breath, 159-180
Simpson, Mona, 109
simplicity, 59-61
Sixth Sense (Nadel), 146
Skiing, 155
Smith, Charles Martin, 65
solitude, 18-19, 22, 103-21
Solitude: A Return to the Self (Storr), 18, 111
Sound and the Fury, The (Faulkner), 181
Spikol, Art, 79, 121
spouses, working at home with, 135-52
State University of New York, 118
statistics:
  homeworkers, 2-9, 143
  telecommuters, 3-4, 6
Storr, Anthony, 18-19, 111
stress, 13-14, 23, 44, 93-94
Suinn, Richard, 157
support systems, 151
survival traits, skills, strengths, 181-192
Survivor Personality, The (Siebert), 181
survivors, 181-192
synchronicity, 39

T

talking to self, 119-20
Talese, Gay, 67
telecommuting, 3-4, 6, 137-38, 149
test, self-assessment, 19-22
Thackeray, William, 181
Theory of Relativity, 161

Third Wave, The (Toffler), 2
Thoreau, Henry David, 107-08
three-question rule, 29-30
Toffler, Alvin, 2, 6

U

Ungerleider, Steven, 154
U.S. News & World Report, 4, 66

V

value system, personal, 31-32
Virgil, 182
"virtual" office, 2-3, 109-10
visualization, 153-180
Visualization (Bry), 157

W

Walden Pond, 104, 108
Wall Street Journal, The, 9, 139, 151-52
Wallace, Don, 144
Washington, George, 41

Webster's New Collegiate Dictionary, 66, 84
Weiner, Leonard, 66
Weiss, Lynn, 49
Weldon, Fay, 68
wellspring, 177-80
Wenner, Jann S., 5
Wilkerson, Isabel, 67
Williams, Tennessee, 151
Willis, Thayer Cheatham, 14, 18
work ethic, 15-17, 41, 70-80, 88
workaholism, 79-80
working hours, regular, 77-78
Working from Home (Edwards), 37
Working Woman, 143
worry, control of, 23-24, 60
Writer, The, 72
writer's block, 100-01
Writer's Digest, 79, 101, 121

Y

Yankelovich Monitor, 5, 8

Z

Zieverink, William, 48-51, 182